INNOCENTS ABROAD...

How Two Baby Boomers Experienced a Cultural
Immersion, the History of Western Art
and Excellent Food on Their Way to
an Extraordinary Year in Europe

JOSEPH W. MCGRATH

INNOCENTS ABROAD...
HOW TWO BABY BOOMERS EXPERIENCED A
CULTURAL IMMERSION, THE HISTORY OF WESTERN
ART AND EXCELLENT FOOD ON THEIR WAY TO
AN EXTRAORDINARY YEAR IN EUROPE

iUniverse books may be ordered through booksellers or by contacting:

iUniverse
1663 Liberty Drive
Bloomington, IN 47403
www.iuniverse.com
1-800-Authors (1-800-288-4677)

ISBN: 978-1-5320-6855-3 (sc)
ISBN: 978-1-5320-6854-6 (e)

Library of Congress Control Number: 2019902257

Print information available on the last page.

iUniverse rev. date: 04/12/2019

DEDICATION

In memory of my dad and mom who inspired me to write. My dad, Joe, left high school as a sophomore to serve in World War II. He had read extensively in his years at sea and, when he returned, immediately tested for and received his GED. He was inspired, through all his reading, to become a writer. He soon met and married my mom, Barbara, who became his champion. While working at Western Electric in manufacturing during the day, he attended Rutgers University at night and, with my mother's assistance in typing and proofreading, graduated in five years as an English major. He wrote prolifically for the next six years and was devastated that he was unable to get anything published. In frustration and to my mom's dismay, he symbolically burned all of his manuscripts in a large heap in our backyard. Dad and Mom, this book is for you.

Our Story

Roma

W e touched down softly at Rome's Leonardo da Vinci airport. My wife Lisa and I were exhilarated and eager to get started. We were finally here. Our adventure was starting right now. A packed bus took our excited, noisy crowd of tourists to the terminal. We waited at the baggage carousel. We knew we had packed far too much. We thought we needed to because it was for all four seasons. All year. But it was still too much. We had four enormous pieces of luggage, two smaller bags and two briefcases. As we dragged them off the carousel one by one, the other passengers looked at us with growing incredulity, pointing at us and whispering. They seemed to be saying, what were these people thinking? Were they moving to Europe for good? We began to wonder, what had we been thinking? Too late now.

We looked like the Keystone Cops trying to drag all this stuff from the carousel through customs to the main terminal area. The wheels on the bags never seemed to cooperate, and we weaved slowly, this way and that, spinning around, and running over our own feet, cussing.

We sailed through immigration, but waiting for our driver seemed like an eternity. Where could he be? Five minutes, 10, 15, 20 minutes went by, and we started to panic. We called our host, Martin, nervously, knowing how little English he spoke. All of our arrangements had been made via email, and they were half-English and half-Italian. We told Martin that our driver hadn't arrived. He spoke in Italian. We spoke slower and louder. He seemed to be saying that he would call the driver and call us back. Wait! Don't hang up!

Shit. Another 15 minutes went by. We thought we were all set with a large Mercedes van, and we could pay with a credit card. Now we might have to scramble and end up taking two separate cabs and have to pay with cash. Did we have enough? We didn't know what it would cost. We didn't know how to get to our Airbnb. We hadn't paid attention to it because we believed the driver would know.

In a confusing second call, Martin kept saying, "O.K., it's O.K." I hoped so. Finally, an hour after we first arrived, a driver appeared with a handwritten sign with our names. He was disheveled: wrinkled black suit, wrinkled white shirt and black tie. He threw our luggage awkwardly on three carts and we dragged them out to a beat-up, old, dirty Opel van. At this point, good enough for us.

A bumpy ride with bad shocks bounced us and our luggage along the A91 motorway, and 35 minutes later we were on the outskirts of Rome. We passed the breathtaking ruins of the Baths of Caracalla and Circus Maximus, the Palatine Hill, the Theater of Marcellus remains and, across from them, the long flight of steps to the magnificent Capitoline Hilltop square designed by Michelangelo. We turned into the Piazza Venezia, the square in front of the monument to King Victor Emmanuel, known by locals as the "wedding cake." The enormous white marble structure with its Corinthian columns, fountains and equestrian statues glowed in the bright sunlight. The centerpiece of this beautiful city. We were really here. We drove around the square past the colossal sculpted Trajan's Column and around the elegant baroque Church of the Gesù.

We turned down our narrow one-way street, Via di Torre Argentina. It was almost as if our driver had weaved us through town on our own private welcome tour. He stopped in front of the large wooden doors we remembered from the Airbnb photos online. We were here.

A small Fiat arrived simultaneously and parked behind us. A young man and a young woman jumped out and began speaking with the driver. It was Martin. Just in time. We had panicked at the airport for no reason at all. This was working out perfectly.

Martin and his girlfriend helped the driver unload our bags and opened the door and waved us into the courtyard beyond. The courtyard we had seen online with gorgeous flowers, plants and blooming trees was now filled with motorcycles, scooters, heaps of dirt and concrete, jigsaw piles of wood pieces, and bags of sand and cement. We asked what had happened, and Martin waved his arms and spoke loudly in Italian. Oh my God, what had we signed up for? Martin then waved to us and began to drag our baggage up the steps.

Being on the fifth floor, we were happy they had an elevator. But Martin and his girlfriend weren't using it. What about the elevator? We opened the door and found out why: It was so small that it couldn't fit two of our big bags and a person at the same time. The bags had to go by themselves, on two trips. We followed him step by step, banging up the countless stairs. I had a feeling this truly was going to be an adventure to remember. Or one we would like to forget.

When we finally had all our luggage upstairs, I had sweated through my shirt. Martin disappeared with Lisa into the kitchen. I wandered into the living room. It didn't look like the pictures, either. There was no table with Champagne and flowers facing the tall window. There was only a single end table next to the couch. The chairs in the photo had become kitchen chairs. The room was spartan. I drifted into the kitchen. It was acceptable, but again not like the pictures. There were no roses to be seen on the pillows in the master bedroom. It was barren.

Where were Lisa and Martin? They were outside on the three-by-four-foot wrought-iron balcony where the tiny washing machine was. Martin was explaining how to use it. Lisa understood maybe 10 percent of what he was saying but kept nodding affirmatively. An outdoor washer. He was then explaining about the dryer. It was a clothesline with 12 clothespins. Great. Anything we asked Martin, he answered, "no problem." He showed Lisa how to use the kitchen appliances. He walked up to me when he was finished and repeated,

"Just like the pictures, just like the pictures." I kept saying, "Not like the pictures!" He smiled broadly and disappeared.

Lisa and I sat at the kitchen table and wondered how we could be so surprised. And I was depressed. I thought I had researched everything thoroughly. We agreed we would go figure it out over a glass of Italian white wine in the restaurant on the ground floor of our building, Vini & Cucina.

We were warmly greeted by Alessandro, a native Roman who spoke excellent English. He is 5-foot-10, a wiry 160 pounds and has close cropped black hair and a five-day beard. Alessandro is funny, sarcastic and always laughing. An Italian Puck. He brought over our wine, a bowl of olives and a basket of those very light and crunchy Italian potato chips. Lisa and he hit it off and quickly became friends. We joked about our crazy arrival and the surprises in our apartment. He told us about himself and the crazy staff and their crowd there. Being a block from the Pantheon, it almost always had tourists as customers. Except for when the Roma soccer games appeared on their multiple televisions, then it was all cheering and screaming locals.

He introduced us to Sylvia, a cute young girl, thin with a short brown shag haircut, who made the pizza there. She was always talking to everyone and always laughing. Lisa and she became famous friends as well, and they hugged and kissed each other every time we arrived or left. Alessandro told us about the owner, Maurizio, who had four children with four different women. Maurizio, we discovered, was handsome, of medium height, with longish salt-and-pepper hair. He always wore jeans, an untucked shirt and a navy-blue sports jacket. He came over to our table several times to say hello before he was distracted by young women. He was always looking to flirt. He would invite himself to every table of young women who came into his place and talk to them in English, Spanish, German or whatever, the entire time they were there. The lucky ones got a free glass of wine.

Maurizio eventually bought us small glasses of grappa. When there were no women around, he would sometimes sit with us and tell us stories filled with wonderful half-English, half-Italian malapropisms that would have made Yogi Berra proud. We quickly forgot about our disappointment with our arrival and the apartment. This small group soon became our close friends and we visited them briefly every day to catch up on Italian, Roman or just restaurant gossip. We thought, what a great first step to feeling like a local, a Roman. This was a wonderful surprise.

The Italian way of life. Martin defined it. When we called to tell him our shower had only cold water, he said no problem, someone would come later that day. When we called the next day, he said no problem, he was busy but would come tomorrow. When we called later that day, he said, no problem, later that week. It was fixed 10 days after our first call. That was a simple problem.

We called Martin to say our gas stove didn't work. He explained that he didn't understand English very well and we would have to call his sister in Alexandria, Va., and she would connect us in a three-way call and translate for us. We called her and explained that our gas stove didn't work. Martin suggested that the gas was out on our entire block. I said that was impossible because the restaurant had gas. He said it must be a problem for the entire building, and I repeated that the restaurant had gas. I asked him to just send a handyman over to diagnose the problem and fix it. He finally acquiesced and agreed to send someone tomorrow. The famous Italian tomorrow. Three days later the handyman arrived. To fix it, he had to hang off our fifth-story balcony. I was worried that if he fell, how long it would take to get the next handyman here in Italy. The funny thing about "Italian time" is that you eventually get used to it. A day can mean a week. A week could be a month. The only thing that is on time in Italy are the trains. And that's possibly a legend.

There was one great thing about our Airbnb, and that was the view. The glass door to our balcony went from the floor to our

12-foot ceiling and was five feet wide. The balcony looked out across Rome but directly at one of its most beautiful churches, Sant'Andrea della Valle, with one of the loveliest and largest domes in the city. Every morning, we woke to see the sun reflecting off this wonderful dome. In the distance to the right we could see the dome of St. Peter's. The rooftop right across from us was a horticultural wonderland of olive trees, flowers and cacti tended to by a slow-moving elderly gentleman. He went out to pick olives every morning in a little hat to protect him from the sun. With our coffee, sitting at the window gazing out and listening to the birds singing from the nearby television antennas was a wonderful way to start our daily adventure.

It was now time to go conquer the city.

THE BIRTH OF A BIG IDEA

I n 2016, Lisa and I retired. Well, sort of retired. Semi-retired. I had retired once before and came back to start my own consulting business, and continued to work fairly long hours the last few years. Lisa retired from Price Waterhouse nearly 30 years before as a manager in its audit practice to successfully raise our three children, Caitlin, Ryan and Brendan – to taxi them, inspect their homework, tutor them, attend their sporting events, bandage them, and nurture them through college. She is a 5-foot-7 perky, perpetually happy brunette who has aged gracefully. I am 5-foot-11, an ex-college football and rugby player with short, gray, curly hair and an impish Irish smile.

With Lisa, almost everything is a great idea, and everyone is her best friend. Every day is the best day of her life. Seriously! Well, at least most of the time. She returned to the workforce as a tax accountant when our last child graduated from college. I was 64 years old and she was 58.

In my life, after graduating from college with a degree in English literature and a minor in theater arts, I spent over 40 years in the information technology business. I saw myself as a hard worker, determined and tenacious. At various times during those years, I was a "wannabe writer," "wannabe painter" and "wannabe sculptor." I occasionally wove courses in each of those disciplines into my schedule, but my focus quickly returned to work.

Our dream over those years was to live for a year in Europe. When we were growing up, we didn't have a junior year abroad like many young students do now. Our children went to England and

Scotland to study, and then to Germany, France, the Netherlands, Ireland and the Czech Republic on breaks. Our children also got to experience summers abroad between their years of college, and added Greece, Switzerland, Iceland and Spain to their travels. We didn't have that opportunity, either.

Most baby boomers, years ago, worked summers and sometimes holiday vacation periods to help pay for college. We certainly did. When we graduated from college, a number of my friends took that summer off to go to Europe before starting their first jobs. Lisa and her sister traveled to Switzerland and Italy for two weeks after her first year with Price Waterhouse. I missed that, too. I couldn't afford it at the time. That is why a year in Europe had been my dream for a long, long time. And now I was semi-retired, and we could finally do it.

I was lucky enough to travel to Europe many times for business, to the U.K., France, Germany, Italy, Switzerland, Austria, Spain, the Netherlands, Belgium and other countries, many of them more than once. It was great. I loved it. But most times, I was in a country for two or three days. I'd fly over, rush around for too many client meetings and dinners, and rush back home to the States. In Paris, I would get brief glimpses of the Eiffel Tower and Notre-Dame from my taxi. The scent of fresh croissants would creep through the taxi window and drift away. I would speed past Rome's Colosseum and peer up through the window only to see it disappear out the back. Sometimes I extended my stay over a long weekend and scurried to see a few of the main attractions. But it was always a rush. I never got to truly enjoy a city, to truly experience its people and its culture. My small adventures were an appetizer but never the main course. Now Lisa and I could finally immerse ourselves in that primordial stew of cultures that helped seed and shape our American spirit. In our new adventure, we could become real Romans, authentic Parisians.

At first, Lisa felt the entire project was a bit daunting. All of the usual concerns. How could we afford it? We weren't fluent in any European language. She spoke and understood only "un peu" of French. Where would we live? How could we accomplish the logistics of moving to multiple countries and cities throughout 12 months, which was our vision? How do you pack for an entire year? All four seasons? How would we navigate the European trains and transportation systems? Health care? Prescription drugs? The list of questions and risks seemed endless. Then suddenly she just relaxed and smiled. Oh come on, let's just do it. We can figure this out.

Research. Research. Research. Good thing we had the internet. It would have taken forever before the digitization of the universe. We bought Michelin green guides for Italy, Germany, Spain, Portugal, Switzerland, the Netherlands, Greece and Austria. They are the gold standard for their one-, two- and three-star ratings of the significant historical sights in Europe. We selected the Red Guide, "Michelin Main Cities of Europe," for its ratings of the best restaurants. Ordered the National Geographic walking tour guides to Paris, Rome, Venice, Barcelona, Berlin and other major cities. Bought Patricia Wells's excellent "Food Lover's Guide to Paris." Printed out the "Best of…" guides to restaurants, cafés, bars and nightclubs from Condé Nast Traveler, Bloomberg and The New York Times. Some of the most up-to-date and insightful writeups were from British newspapers like The Telegraph and The Guardian, and from London's Time Out.

We triangulated the reviews to see what appeared in multiple recommendations, and stacked all of this craziness in piles high on my desk, the kitchen table and the kitchen counter. We made binders of the results by city and by country, and sorted them repeatedly to create our Master Plan. It was making Lisa crazy but she stayed calm, went patiently with the flow, and was supportive of this insane intergalactic multi-country effort. I was persistent and persuasive, and my passion became her reassurance that it would ultimately happen. Probably haphazardly, but it would happen.

We questioned some of our better-traveled friends, but no one had ever been away in multiple countries this long. People who had stayed for long periods had gone to a single country where they had

THE MASTER PLAN

Lisa and I needed the right combination of structure and flexibility for our trip. The right mix of security and safety balanced with the freedom to be spontaneous. We started our thinking and planning around the three countries that we were most passionate about: Italy, France and Spain. We believed they were the most passionate and emotional of the European people, people we could connect most easily with, and become friends with. Our three anchor cities would then be Rome, Paris and Barcelona. We would use these as our bases to explore the rest of the country.

Next we began with living arrangements. We researched the most central locations in each of these cities. We plotted them on Google maps, then explored other travelers' favorite neighborhoods. We wanted to walk everywhere, no cars, subways or taxis, to experience every city, neighborhood by neighborhood, street by street, and get to know them intimately.

We decided on Airbnbs for each of these cities for three months each. When we went to explore other cities, we could leave our big suitcases behind and have a home to come back to. We researched each city's options, listing after listing. The Rome apartment we selected was about equal distance from the Trevi Fountain, the Piazza Navona and the Piazza Venezia. Paris's was in St.-Germain-des-Prés, a block from Boulevard St.-Germain, the Café de Flore and Les Deux Magots. We were a few short blocks from the Seine, the Louvre and Notre-Dame. The flat in Barcelona was across from the Port Vell harbor front and anchored in the back corner of the historic and fascinating Gothic Quarter.

We decided to add Airbnbs in Florence, Siena and Seville to extend our network of apartments and give us some comfort so we wouldn't be deciding too much on the fly when we were finally over in Europe. The rest of our side trips would be ad-hoc and we would stay in hotels. And then we wanted to complete the year by going to Russia, and to Ukraine and Belarus, where my mom's parents were born.

We also developed a master plan that was a framework for each day's activities. We would divide each day into quadrants: exercise, lunch, touring and then a relaxing café.

The first thing we would do upon arriving would be to join a gym in every city and head over there every morning immediately after coffee. We thought that with Europe's rich food we would need it, running every day and lifting weights every other day. Then, after returning home and showering, we would make lunch our big meal of the day. We would have no breakfast and no dinner.

I researched restaurants extensively, and we would schedule every lunch a week ahead to make sure we had reservations. Disregarding all of the guidebooks and local customs, we would always arrive immediately after they opened at 12 p.m. Being there first, we would get to know the staff, order a bottle of wine and sparking water, and have time to discuss the menu extensively with our server and understand each restaurant's specialties. We would avoid all of the common tourist complaints about being ignored by the waiters, slow service and running out of their specialty dishes. We would spend two and a half hours over lunch, enjoy every dish thoroughly, eating leisurely, and Lisa would engage our fellow patrons in conversation. Every day would be great and full of travel networking.

From there we would begin our touring schedule, limited to two hours a day so we would never get overloaded or overwhelmed. We also would be able to spend enough time to truly understand everything we saw and understand its historical significance. Our Michelin green guides would be invaluable here. In some museums, like the Louvre, we would explore it, buy the book about it, and return to explore all over again. For the Louvre, we would see if we could even buy an annual pass.

Finally, after returning home and a brief nap, we would go out to explore a café every evening for a glass or two of wine. We would find our favorites and return to lively discussions with the bartenders, servers and their regular local patrons. In some cafés, we would try to become friends with a number of locals. The sociable Lisa would again be key here. These new friends would help integrate us into the city and give us their own lists of new favorites to explore.

We hoped this master plan would give us a daily cadence that would weave all of the new crazy adventures and sights we would experience into a structured approach. It would be our mantra, the discipline that would make everything work. It was perfect.

How to Budget for a Year in Europe

The first thing to plan for is a year of housing. As I knew from experience, couples rent their homes to families or individuals in business relocations all the time. You should start working with a local real estate agent to determine what you might be able to rent your home for. Use that estimate to begin a search for what you can afford in an Airbnb rental. You would be surprised to find Airbnb rentals as inexpensive as $20 a day in Rome, Paris and Barcelona. I'm pretty sure you wouldn't want to stay there, but they are available. We rented for higher prices — but remember, you will be out and about, touring, eating, people-watching and drinking wine or coffee in grand parks, at the beach, and on vistas overlooking your favorite cities most of every day, and you don't need to spend a fortune on housing.

When we were looking at housing options, we found ample choices for $100 a day in Rome and Paris, and around $80 a day in Barcelona. At a time when even a Holiday Inn in Kansas City is at least $99, I am confident that if you select the right city in Europe and are flexible, you can find something that meets your budget. We actually spent less on Airbnbs than what we rented our condo for. It worked out perfectly for us.

How about the cost of the flights that get you there? The low-cost air travel revolution in Europe has surpassed even the U.S. price reductions. Norwegian Air had some real bargains from the U.S. to Europe and was rated as a customer satisfaction leader. In

2018, flights to Rome from Kennedy Airport in New York were $602, to Paris $530, and to Barcelona $553. Round trip! All were direct flights. We took Norwegian, and the flight and crew were great. We booked business class seats that were less expensive than coach seats on most American airlines and were treated to excellent food and drinks and extremely friendly service. "Tusen takk" to our Norwegian friends.

Finally, we planned the cost of our daily meals by pooling a year's worth of our traditional U.S. expenses from supermarkets, restaurants, liquor stores and in our case, club dues (golf or social). We divided that number by the number of days we would be in Europe and that was our daily expense target. (We took a leave of absence from our clubs.) In reality, we exceeded that number some days and cut back other days. An expensive Paris restaurant was offset by an inexpensive trattoria in Rome or tapas bar in Barcelona. It worked out perfectly.

Our gym dues in Europe were offset by cancelling our gym memberships in the U.S. We consciously decided we would do no shopping for clothing, art or crafts to take home, or any other extra purchases. Our train transportation was offset by not having gasoline expenses or insurance for our cars. The major net additions were the few travel guides we bought, the admission fees we paid and a few violations of our "no clothing" rule such as Lisa's Italian fedora, French beret and vibrant Spanish flamenco dress. They were the only increases in our annual budget, in addition to our air travel over to Europe.

We took all of this and created an overall budget by country by week. We kept thinking we were forgetting something but in reality we were roughly right. This crazy dream of ours was going to work without breaking the bank. Incredible.

THE LONG–TERM VISA

W e were all set. We had committed to three-month Airbnbs in our three favorite cities: Rome, Paris and Barcelona. Excellent. Then I encountered an incredible surprise that we were sure would turn out to be a disaster. We could stay in the European Union for only 90 days with our U.S. passports. How did we not know that? How was that possible? That's crazy.

The U.S./E.U. Schengen regulations allowed us only three months before we had to leave. Then we had to remain out of Europe for another 90 days before we could return. Oh my God! What a foolish mistake to make. Why three months? What is magical about three months? I quickly checked and found that we couldn't back out of any of our Airbnb reservations without a major financial penalty.

I scoured the embassy websites of Italy, the first stop on our journey, for any possible exception. I first found the website of the Italian Consulate. Naturally it was in Italian. Consolato Generale d'Italia Filadelfia. Great. Why would an Italian website in the United States be in Italian? I found three different websites for them, all in Italian. Finally, I found an English version of the website. And there it was, something called a long-term visa. It would allow you to stay for 12 months. Excellent. The solution!

Although much of this website was also in Italian, I found enough details that explained that you could get this visa if you were staying with Italian relatives, or if you were going to college in Italy or had a full-time job there. Another possibility was if you owned a home in Italy or were part of a U.S. military unit stationed there. I couldn't find anything about tourists. I might have just missed it. I called a telephone number listed on the website. It was a recorded message in Italian. I tried another number. This recording was in English, and I left a long, detailed message explaining our situation. Nobody called back. I called many more times, and those calls weren't returned, either. The Italian Consulate in Philadelphia, where we live, was open from 9 a.m. to noon on Mondays, Wednesdays and Fridays. I rushed over. I still had an hour before they closed.

When I arrived, there was no clear indication where the visa office was. I rushed around searching for it. Finally I found it. The waiting room was empty and I raced up to the window. I explained my challenge to the clerk. He told me to call the number on the website to get an appointment. I told him that I had called. Could he get me one? No, he said, call the number. I begged him to explain how we could make this work, and get long-term visas as tourists. He told me what I had already gleaned from the website: students, full-time workers, U.S. military personnel. If you owned a home it was possible, or if you were going to live with relatives who were native Italians. I was sure he was mistaken. Not allowing tourists was crazy.

I went home and downloaded from the Italian website all the forms required for the visa. I had a cramp in the pit of my stomach. I had a feeling that it just wasn't possible. I went to the website of the French Embassy in Washington, found the long-term visa section and downloaded all of the forms there as well. Those were in English, and it appeared that France might allow a long-term tourist visa. I then went to the website of the Spanish Embassy in New York and downloaded all of their forms as well. The Spanish rules on tourist visas were unclear.

The collective requirements were overwhelming. The countries wanted copies of our passports and driver's licenses, a notary-approved proof of our assets and net worth, copies of our bank statements, proof of international medical coverage (which we didn't have), a letter from our doctor stating that we were of good mental health and free of contagious diseases and drug addiction, and our prior year tax returns. They also needed our marriage certificate.

France and Spain needed a notary-approved payment statement that proved you had rented an apartment there. Spain needed copies of our fingerprints and a certification from the F.B.I. that we had no arrest data in its files. France also required one letter explaining the purpose of our trip and another letter stating that we did not intend to engage in any paid professional activity that required a work permit. Good grief. It was probably easier to get into these countries as a refugee.

How were we going to get all of this done in the time window we had before we were scheduled to leave for Rome? We were due there on Oct. 1, and here it was July and we had already sublet our condo. This was insane! Our research indicated that we stood the best chance with the French. We quickly set up visits at the French Embassy in Washington and, for backup, the Spanish Embassy in New York, and bought our train tickets. The earliest appointments were three weeks away. We had a very tight window. If these visits didn't work, our entire vacation would be finished before it started. We were dying! We quickly began the process to work with our local police department to send our fingerprints to the F.B.I. We called insurance companies about international health insurance, which included coverage for emergency evacuation and the return of mortal remains. We had to collect this voluminous amount of information in a maniacal timeframe.

A few weeks later the forms were completed. We had copies made for all three countries, which included our photographs. We started with our local Italian Consulate. Called multiple times for an appointment. No one called back. We just showed up during office hours. They told us they required an appointment. This was theater of the absurd. Forget it, we would move on to our appointment at the French Embassy in Washington. By now we were getting really anxious.

We arrived at 11 o'clock for our 11:30 appointment. The grounds were heavily guarded and security was tight. At the main guardhouse entrance to the embassy property, they asked to see our receipt for our appointment booking. The guard looked at it, logged it and asked Lisa, "Where is yours?"

I responded that the appointment was for both of us. He was abrupt. "You need one for each of you," he declared.

I explained that I had signed up for each of us separately and there must be a mistake.

"Sorry," he responded. "She cannot go in with you."

A shiver ran down my spine. Every time I believed we had cleared an insurmountable barrier, we found another. My head was spinning. I thought I had signed both of us up. But had I? I had one of those out-of-body experiences, when your eyes go out of focus and you hear everyone speaking very slowly. Lisa was talking to the guard in rudimentary French, but her voice sounded as if it were coming from a tunnel. How had I blown it again?

The next thing I knew, we both had passes to the embassy and were walking up the long cement path to the building. I asked Lisa what had happened. She explained simply, he is a Frenchman and I am a woman. O.K.

We entered and were directed to the room for the long-term visas. It was packed. Servicemen and their families, students, businessmen and businesswomen. You take a numbered ticket and wait for three different sets of clerks at 20 different windows. First you pay for the visa, even before they examine your paperwork and commit to approving it. They don't return your money if you aren't approved. At the second window your paperwork is examined, and at the third you find out if you were conditionally approved. Conditionally? That made us a bit uncomfortable. Time was marching on and we knew they closed at noon.

We were really on edge. We were worried that we stated we were going to Paris on Oct. 1 when our first stop was actually Rome. We weren't going to Paris until Jan. 1, and you couldn't apply earlier than 60 days before you arrived. We would not be conforming to this rule. If they caught us were we finished? We hadn't filled out that part of the form, and we quietly argued what we should do. I panicked and told Lisa to just write that we were going on Oct. 1 even though our rental agreement said Jan. 1. In the middle of our whispered but intense discussion, Lisa dropped all of our papers. They flew all over the floor and across the room. Like little children, we scrambled back and forth on our knees between everyone's chairs and picked everything up. Now our hearts were really racing! Just fill out the date as Oct. 1, I pleaded. Lisa did and we were immediately called by the payment clerk.

We walked up, and the clerk repeated what the guard had said: They would process the visa only for the person with the official appointment. Another chill ran down my spine. We were finished. Could the goofy trick with the Frenchman and the woman smiling, flirting and speaking awkward French work again? A miracle occurred. It did.

The clerk took our money and we sat back down. The people ahead of us were all speaking in French and laughing with the other clerks. The office closed at noon. We weren't going to make it. Another panic! Lisa told me to chill. It would all work out. We were finally called at 11:55. Our paperwork was in order and they asked us to sit down. Time ticked away. We were the last ones there.

We were called to the last window. They told us we were conditionally approved. We had to hand them our passports, and when we received final approval the visas would be stapled to our passports and they would send them back to us in the mail. In the mail? Oh no! What if they are not approved? What If they get lost in the mail and we didn't have our passports for our backup meeting with the Spanish Embassy? We had to bet the entire trip on the French. Oh no!

We left, caught a cab to Union Station and had a stiff drink. Our die was cast. We would just have to wait to see if it all worked out. The only thing left to do was chill.

Two nervous weeks later, both passports with attached visas did indeed arrive in the mail. Our European adventure was saved. Game on.

EQUIPPED FOR EUROPE

I f you are a seasoned traveler or have gone to Europe often over the years, many of our recommendations should be second nature. The difference might just be in how things change when it's a very long visit. Some of the things we thought were important were an activity tracker, international insurance, a year's worth of prescriptions, the ability to listen to a wide range of music and watch different educational television shows or DVDs, and finally, sufficient power adapters.

One of the most important new purchases we made were activity trackers. They count the steps you walk and stairs you climb, and monitor your heart rate and the quality of your sleep. We had set a minimum target of 10,000 steps per day. That was to ensure we had sufficient heart-healthy activity and could keep our weight down with all of that rich Italian, French and Spanish food. After some research, Lisa and I selected Fitbit watches. An Apple watch is another good option for activity tracking. Both devices have additional applications, including one that can monitor sleep. Ten thousand steps a day was an important benchmark. We almost always exceeded it, often by a lot when our workouts were included. Actually, by the time we returned home, we calculated that we had walked the equivalent of New York City to Salt Lake City. The real benefit was that we had gained no weight over the course of our adventure. After we returned home, well, that's another story.

The second important thing we did was convince our doctor that we needed to bring a year's worth of our medical prescriptions. Initially he was reluctant, but then he agreed. Lisa needed only her blood pressure medicine, while I needed blood pressure medicine and Celebrex – I have arthritis from too many years of playing rugby. One can make a counter-argument that prescription drugs are always cheaper in Europe, but we didn't want to take a chance on their availability. We did the same thing with Prilosec and Allegra because we weren't sure we could get the identical products. If you don't want to carry them around, you can have a family member periodically mail them to you, but we were always concerned about receiving mail unless we rented a mailbox at a post office or a mailbox service.

International health insurance was required for our French long-term visa, and we found a special insurance broker for that. We were pleased that the cost was reasonable, under $300 each. Be sure to get the option that allows you to be flown back to the United States in the case of a serious emergency. We also kept our U.S. insurance for that reason. And get the provision that covers the return of mortal remains, just in case.

For music, do not assume that your host has effective equipment or reception, or that there will be any range of stations. You can use your PC or iPad as the source, but we also brought an Amazon Echo speaker to improve the sound quality. It made a big difference. Also check to see if your digital streaming music station is available in Europe. We were surprised that Pandora was not available, but we were lucky that we had also subscribed to Spotify. It was great to wake up to it every morning and listen just before bed.

In terms of television, even if it is advertised as available, assume the worst. Most hosts have the minimum package from their cable providers. It Italy, there were two channels that showed reruns of "NCIS" and "Blue Bloods" in English. But after the very long commercial breaks, the show might resume in Italian. Very fluky. We subscribed to both Netflix and Amazon Prime. We didn't watch much TV at our apartments, but we did on our iPhones while we were running on the elliptical at the gym.

Amazon Prime was invaluable as well for getting up to speed on many of the artists whose work we were seeing. While in Rome, I watched the entire "Art of the Western World" series. In Paris, I watched the Great Courses programs on the Louvre and other DVDs and downloads on the Impressionists, Degas, Renoir and "Cézanne et Moi." In Amsterdam, Rembrandt and van Gogh. You get the picture. Just remember to bring a set of Bluetooth headphones. We also brought a small, inexpensive DVD player that plugged into our PC.

Everyone knows that electrical adapters are critical in Europe, but you may not recognize how many you actually need. Apartments might provide one at the most. But you should plan on having one for each device you bring. And a Google Translator app for your iPhone will be invaluable if you need to run out to a hardware store for more.

You may want to bring a money belt to use while you're out walking. The major tourist attractions of Europe draw the highest concentration of pickpockets. And so do the subways. We didn't buy anything special, but we never carried a wallet or a purse. We took sufficient money for each day in our zippered pocket and a single credit card — Visa or MasterCard because not all European establishments accept American Express. We used a MasterCard with no foreign transaction fees — and we made sure to inform the credit card company and our bank that we were heading out of the country.

FAMILY AND FRIENDS

There was another set of issues we had to think through before we left for Europe. Would our parents be in good hands over our year away? And would our children be all right as well?

My dad died a number of years ago of cancer. Lisa's father had died recently, but she and her sisters are very close and they supported one another warmly and thoughtfully through the grieving period.

Lisa's mom, Charlotte, 83, was now in assisted living in a retirement home very close to Lisa's sister Susan's home in Hershey, Pa. The sisters all knew the nursing staff well and believed they were attentive and competent. Charlotte also had a personal assistant who helped her with shopping, writing letters and other odd jobs. It was working very well for her.

My mom, Barbara, was a spunky, independent 87-year-old. She traveled between her modest retirement homes at the New Jersey shore and southern Florida. She flew back and forth each year to catch up with her golf friends, painting friends, cruise ship friends, card-playing friends, shuffleboard friends and dinner theater friends. They were all mostly women because their husbands had passed away. She was always very busy.

While my mother was in New Jersey, my brother Tom and his wife, Holly, visited her almost every other week and often drove her to northern New Jersey for weekends at their home near a lake.

When Barbara was in Florida, my cousin Victor and his wife, Libby, were with her nearly every week. They were slightly younger than my mom.

In between, my mom caught up with her children via video conferencing on FaceTime using an iPad my brother Charlie had bought her as a gift. We would use FaceTime to stay in contact with her on our trip. This wonderful, hyperactive, feisty old woman would be fine. She packed four or five different activities with different sets of friends into every single day of her life.

We were sure our children would be fine as well. Our oldest, Caitlin, 27, was in Washington, having left her job at the USO in fund-raising, and was back in college on a fast track to be a nurse. It would be her dream job. She was dating a very nice Marine Corps lawyer who was working at the Pentagon. Our middle child, Ryan, 25, was happy in his job in customer relations and dating a wonderful young woman in medical school. Our youngest, Brendan, 23, was working hard in New York City in investment banking and had a very nice girlfriend in banking as well. We were confident everyone was in a good place.

Our big choice on the issue of friends and family was whether we should rent one-bedroom or two-bedroom apartments in Europe. After surveying our children, our brothers and sisters, our current friends and our high school and college friends, we decided we should go for it. Two bedrooms. Everyone we asked was interested in spending a week if we would be there for a year. Great. What a mixed-up mosaic of fun for everyone. A cornucopia, a patchwork quilt, of different friends and family from every episode of our lives.

Big lesson learned there. Of my two brothers, only Charlie could actually make it. He joined us in Paris. After thinking it through, my brother Tom was concerned that Holly's health might become an issue. He had to decline.

Of Lisa's three sisters, Ellen joined us in Barcelona for a fun-filled weekend of beachside clubs and tapas-hopping at the end of a business trip. Her sister Susan was concerned about leaving her three young girls behind, and her sister Alice had committed to another Europe trip with her best friend.

My college friend Jack joined us with his wife, Barbara, as part of a longer vacation. Another set of friends, the Reillys, whom we had known through our son Brendan's lacrosse team in college, joined us for a weekend. It was another great, whirling, fun-filled, mix of our favorite art-filled churches and trattorias.

Our daughter, Caitlin, made it to Paris for an entire week, and it was an extraordinary experience for us all. She was our tour guide at the Louvre, the Musée d'Orsay, Notre-Dame, Sainte-Chapelle, the Arc de Triomphe, the Champs-Elysées, Les Invalides, the Panthéon and Sacré-Coeur. She had been there before and was a touring machine. (She is also a marathon runner.) She found an excellent artist on the hilltop at Montmartre, near Sacré-Coeur, who painted her portrait as she sat under an umbrella in the rain at night. It is one of her favorite possessions and now hangs framed in her apartment. She also accompanied us to all of our favorite restaurants.

Our son Ryan made a trip to Rome and it was delightful. He went with our tour guide, Rosa Militano, to visit the Vatican, St. Peter's, the Sistine Chapel and the Vatican Museum. He joined us at the Colosseum, the Roman Forum, the Pantheon, the Trevi Fountain, the Piazza Navona and our favorite churches. He also visited our favorite restaurants. Ryan joined us a second time with his girlfriend, Brie, in Barcelona, and that was a fabulous experience as well. They explored the city on their own.

Our younger son, Brendan, had his Rome trip, then his Paris trip, then his Barcelona trip cancelled by his investment banking directors because he was needed on important deals. He had been to London, Prague and Dublin before, but was eager to experience these new cities. He was disappointed but we all understood.

It was, all told, an extraordinary experience, to be in Europe with our children, even if they couldn't all be there at the same time. And we were otherwise in constant contact with our children, brothers, sisters and moms. We emailed them daily on a mass distribution list, sent all of our photographs, used WhatsApp messaging in between, and FaceTime for my mom. Lisa sent postcards to her mom, Charlotte.

But while everyone we asked agreed that Paris, Rome and Barcelona sounded like great fun and expressed interest, they could not commit to it months in advance. Everyone had important, legitimate reasons. So the lesson was learned: lower your expectations. Plan only for yourself. Our second bedroom was occupied only 18 percent of the time.

One would be better off to rent a place for friends and family in an inexpensive hotel nearby, or put them on the couch. Our overall budget would have had a very different profile if we had known this ahead of time. But no harm, no foul.

THE THREAD THAT WOULD CONNECT EVERYTHING

Before our journey we bought a few educational courses in preparation for the trip. We bought the Rosetta Stone DVD to try to learn basic Italian. From a company called The Great Courses, we got "The Smithsonian Guide to Essential Italy" and "A History of European Art." We were both neophytes in these subjects.

After reviewing the outline of the art history course, we had an epiphany. Our biggest surprise of this journey through Western Europe would be that there was an amazing thread that would connect everything we would do. That thread was that we had unknowingly selected our Airbnbs to follow the evolution of Western art across the continent. Step by step. It was not always perfectly linear, but it was very close. We had no intention of pursing this specifically; it was a coincidence that our travels would take us down this path. In a sense, we would be traveling from 509 B.C. and ancient Rome to the early Middle Ages, the Romanesque period, Gothic, early Renaissance, high Renaissance, Baroque, Romanticism, Realism, Impressionism, Post-Impressionism, Expressionism and Cubism, which would deliver us through a 2,450-year journey in time to Surrealism in the 1950s. The scheduling of our Airbnbs would take us from Rome to Siena and Florence. Rome to Paris. Paris to Barcelona. And Barcelona to Seville and back.

Our plan would now be to visit every major coliseum, amphitheater, museum, church, baptistery and monument on this journey. We planned to seek them out in Italy, France, the

Netherlands and Spain. Our Airbnb residences would follow this thread of the evolving history of art, sculpture and architecture through those 2,400-plus years.

We would be able to see how these artists and architects would influence one another over the course of time. How each genre evolved. It was the first time that this history and its evolution would all make sense to us. The continuum of scientific and cultural influence on it as well. We would see how it was driven by the rise and fall of economies and their associated political city/states, and how these artists moved among countries amid plagues, wars and revolutions. We would understand how artists thrived under the patronage of emperors, popes, cardinals, kings, princes, wealthy trade guilds, and eventually wealthy citizens. It would be a fascinating education driven by art, which in turn would also educate us about the other cultural and historical developments in those countries at those times.

Architecture and art are not the only threads that could connect the important centers of a travel agenda. One could follow the path of the great composers and travel from Baroque to Classical, Romantic to Modernist. Or follow the evolution of literature, philosophy, government or democracy, or even wine. But our adventure, by a fantastic and weird coincidence of scheduling our living arrangements, would be an incredibly exciting one. By the time we returned, we would visit 45 museums and 55 churches in 20 cities and four countries along 40 train segments following this thread. The history of Western Art would be the thread that would connect everything.

Parallel Lives

As we looked forward to our adventure, Lisa and I paused, took a breath or two, and reflected. Although we had been happily married for 30 years, we had lived parallel lives. I was passionate about my career, and about making a difference in business. Lisa had made a decision, early in our marriage, that the greatest potential joy in her life would be as a full-time mother. It was a plan on which we agreed.

Over the next 30 years, I worked hard to support our family and get ahead. I wasn't always the smartest guy in the room, but I tried to be the hardest working. As an executive at a leading information technology consulting company and four Fortune 500 firms, I was promoted 14 times.

We accepted every new career opportunity. Strategy, marketing, sales, product planning, product development, general management — every turn was new, instructive and exciting, and I jumped at them. But each step also presented challenges, and more work — often 65- to 70-hour weeks. In particular, the turnarounds of a few businesses that were losing money were emotionally exhausting and personally scarring as the companies let people go to become profitable again.

Many of these opportunities also required us to move, to Stamford, Conn.; Palo Alto, Calif.; Rochester, N.Y.; Blue Bell, Pa. They required significant travel as well — to Asia, Latin America, Europe and every major U.S. city, taking up 40 to 60 percent of my time. When we relocated, I often lived alone in our new destination for four or five months in a Residence Inn while Lisa would manage the process of selling our home and moving the children to a new school.

Eventually I started my own consulting company, but this meant traveling — primarily in the U.S. — from Sunday night to Friday evening.

The skills I acquired over those years — vision, detailed planning, the ability to adapt quickly to change and a strong attention to execution — would serve me well on our forthcoming trip.

Lisa, meanwhile, raised three wonderful and successful children, Caitlin, Ryan and Brendan. She nurtured and navigated them through swim team, soccer, field hockey, softball, baseball, lacrosse, wrestling, ski racing, track, basketball, golf, tennis and tae kwon do. To this she added piano, ballet, art classes and band (drums, viola, violin and oboe).

Lisa also oversaw our children's homework, edited their papers, attended all of their sporting events, and served as president of the PTA. She sent the kids off to the slopes of Mount Hood in Oregon, Whistler in Canada and Saas-Fee in Switzerland for summer ski race camps. She ensured that every available week in the summer was filled with other sports camps for all three, and for Caitlin, Johns Hopkins and Oxford University educational camps as well. Was she a helicopter mother? No, closer to an armed drone mother.

Lisa was shy and introverted from her childhood through high school but started to blossom in college. With our frequent moves and the demands of my travel, she became a passionate networker in support of herself and our children, collaborating with teachers, principals, parents of classmates, Little League coaches and parents of teammates, as well as with neighbors. Her network reach encircled our entire community in each town we lived in. It made her feel stable, connected and secure. And it built skills that would prove invaluable to us in Europe.

For all the years I was working, I was home and conscious only from 8 to 11 p.m., if I was lucky. I worked most Saturdays, often taking one of our children with me.

It was really only on Sundays that Lisa and I had extensive time together, enjoying her wonderful omelette breakfast spreads, Bloody Marys and mimosas, the Sunday New York Times, classical music, and eventually watching whichever was our new favorite local football team. We also had wonderful one-week summer vacations with our children to destinations along the East and West Coasts.

But Lisa and I were now going to spend 24 hours a day, seven days a week with each other for 12 months. We loved each other, but the last 30 years had not prepared us for that. Did we really know what the year had in store for us? We would soon find out.

LISA: THE GLUE AND THE GREASE

When we went to Europe, we had a passionate desire to become locals: real Romans, Parisians, Barcelonians. We wanted to absorb their cultures, behavior, thoughts and emotions. We just didn't quite know how to accomplish it. We had very little language skills, outside of basic French. Then it just happened. Lisa made it happen.

Lisa has always been very inquisitive, with a genuine interest in people. All people. She explored the people we encountered, their relationships, their family, their culture and way of life. Whenever we were in a restaurant, wine bar, brasserie, tapas bar, wine store, gym, wherever, she reached out to everyone within speaking distance.

Lisa asked about their girlfriends, boyfriends, husbands, wives and children. She asked where they lived. How long was their commute? Did they take a bus, car, scooter or bicycle? How did they like their job? How passionate were they about their city's soccer team? Where did they shop for clothes? Food?

If we frequented a place, she really got to know them, and they us. If they were under 30, she adopted them. She built the connective tissue across a network of relationships in every major city we spent significant time in. She made every place we went into "Cheers," the old television series, where everyone knew everyone in that neighborhood bar in Boston.

Lisa found out what major sites they had visited in their towns. (Which was mostly none, though they had lived there their entire lives.) She tried to talk them out of smoking. Gave them coaching on their significant other. We took some out to dinner. Many got in trouble with "the boss" for talking to her so often (and for so long).

From all these encounters we discovered the best-kept secrets in local bars, wine stores and family restaurants. She talked Sabrina, our Barcelona Airbnb owner, into bringing us fresh fruit and vegetables from her farm. Sabrina also bought us the perfect tickets in the shade to the Seville bullfights when we couldn't understand the website and weren't able to navigate it in Spanish.

Because of Lisa, we became close friends with Marco, Paolo, Giancarlo, Lara, Diego, Alessandro, Sylvia and Maurizio in Italy. Juan, Max, Matthieu, Patty, Sophie, Pierre-Eric and Evelyne in France. José, Basam, José Maria, Eric and Sabrina in Spain. We have photographs of the two of us hugging all of them. Too many friends to remember them all.

The key to being woven into the fabric of a society is to engage with and care about its people. Not just inquire and explore. Ask. Listen. Care. That's how Lisa became the glue and grease as we were temporarily transformed into real Europeans.

THE COMMUNIST BAR

W e read about it in The Guardian, in an article titled "10 of the Best Bars in Rome." "This place takes you back to what neighborhood Roman wine bars used to be," the newspaper said. It described the patrons as an eclectic combination of writers, architects, artists, poets and old hippie types – primarily middle-aged Romans with a few curious tourists sprinkled in. It sounded compelling. We had to go. It was near the Campo de' Fiori.

The bar was called Il Vinaietto, and it was a bit difficult to find. And when we finally found it, we thought we were mistaken: no sign, an aging stucco exterior, and two sets of rusting green doors on either side with bright circular white lights illuminating the dark street. Inside, the room was a large horseshoe, with the bar across the front wall just inside the two doors. The floor was covered in 1950ish black-and-white checked tiles. There was one tall refrigerator in the center of the horseshoe opposite the bar for self-serve beer, and another, for wine, on one side. The rest of the walls were lined floor to ceiling with dust-covered wine bottles. This was one of Rome's top 10 bars?

It was 7 in the evening when we arrived, and the bar was very, very crowded. There was a large group of people outside drinking in the small one-way street. Several small groups stood laughing, gesturing and talking very loudly. Cars had to crawl by them, but the drinkers ignored the cars edging through.

Inside there were about five small, low, granite-topped tables surrounded by small chairs on either side of the bar that dominated the front of the room. A number of groups had pulled together

35

empty wine crates to create their own tables and chairs. We had to slide around these groups to even get in the place. Mainly Italian wines were on offer, although a few patrons drank Italian beer out of bottles. There was a small chalkboard menu on the wall that described the eight wines available. They were all three or four euros per glass.

A tough-looking older woman with long, dark, wavy hair was tending bar. She wore a black dress with a colorful blue scarf and scowled at the customers when they pointed to the wine list to order. We got up the courage to do the same. She scowled at us, too, pretending not to understand, and then served us what she wanted and collected our cash. We were happy to get our wine and retreated to the back to observe the scene.

Two older men appeared to be in charge. One was tired-looking, a pony-tailed, gray-haired, gray-mustached and bearded hippie with wire-rimmed glasses. He was constantly carrying crates of wine, Prosecco and beer up a set of skinny stairs from the basement. We later found out his name was Giancarlo. The other was a stylish gentleman, also with longish, well-coifed salt and pepper hair, who was chatting up customers at the far end of the bar. He was talking and frequently laughing and brushing his hand through his hair. We found out that he was Marco, and that they were indeed partners and owners.

We scanned the room and noticed something unusual. All of the pictures and posters on the walls were of Communist icons. A large poster of Che Guevara stared out at us from the back wall. A colorful yellow Mao Zedong watched us from another. We walked around the back perimeter to find a young Fidel Castro, and a poster of Mussolini with a big red "No" hand-painted across his face. On a far wall was a large poster that said "PCI" — Partito Comunista Italiano — and "Vota Comunista" in big red letters.

We stopped at a large collection of black and white pictures, apparently from the 1960s, of long-haired men and women organizing and speaking to a similarly long-haired crowd. Many were holding large flags on tall staffs. Three individuals were the focus of all of the photos. Could these could be the infamous Communist rallies of Rome that made Europeans so uneasy in the 1960s? Maybe this was the critical clue to this mysterious place. Could the two owners and the tough bartender be the people in the photos? We named this crazy place the Communist Bar, and we decided it was fascinating. The wine was excellent and the price was very fair. We decided we would become regulars in this strange place while we were in Rome.

On our third visit, a guest joined us at our small table. He had a lightweight black leather jacket, brown glasses, short black hair, and a black mustache and beard, and had a sort of knapsack on his back. He placed his motorcycle helmet in the center of our table, sat down on the extra chair, and asked us in English with a thick Italian accent, "American?"

"Yes," we replied.

"We don't get many Americans here, mostly only locals," he said. He initiated a long, animated discussion with us about American politics, Italian politics and a host of other subjects. He had strong opinions on each area we discussed. He made a guttural sound and tilted his head sideways every time he disagreed. We finally got around to asking him about the two owners, the bartender and the black and white photos on the wall.

"Marco and Giancarlo, yes," he said. "In the late 1960s and early 1970s, they were two of the leaders of the Rome chapter of the Italian Communist Party. In the days after World War II, the party was the second-biggest political party in Italy, with the support of 34 percent of all voters in the mid-'70s. At one point, Italy had the largest Communist Party in the West, with over two million members."

"And the woman bartender?" we inquired.

"Lara, she was Marco's girlfriend in those days. They broke up years ago, but they remained friends ever since."

"Are they still Communists?" we asked.

"No. In the late 1970s and 1980s, the Italian Communist Party broke away from its affiliation with Moscow and became socialist.

Marco later became a postman and Giancarlo became the leader of the Italian meat-cutters union. Marco's father bought this bar for his older brother, who decided this life wasn't for him. Marco was asked to take it over and he asked Giancarlo to help him run it. They have been together ever since."

"Everyone seems to know each other here," we said. "Everyone speaks only Italian here, and we always feel a bit lost. Is everyone here a regular?"

"Yea, essentially. That's why I came over, to figure you two out. Welcome. My name is Diego," he said. "I am hardly ever here."

We thanked him for stopping by. "You have made this place even more interesting," we concluded.

As we began to go there more often, it turned out that Diego was there every day.

The next time we were there, Diego came by to introduce a friend of his, another regular, Paolo. He wore a sweater-vest, and had a cherubic face, a receding hairline, and a pair of glasses with one arm missing. He seemed to be eternally happy and upbeat. He explained that he was part of Marco and Giancarlo's team when they traveled across Italy to find undiscovered wines. He said his family were once the largest and most successful silversmiths in Italy. As times changed and the work went offshore, it became too expensive to compete and they had to close the business. He grew sad as he spoke. It had been in his family for years.

"Paolo, why are the wines excellent but have such reasonable prices?" we inquired.

"Because Marco and Giancarlo are still Communists at heart," he explained.

"I don't get it," I said.

"They believe that this is the "Roman people's bar," and everyone here are their friends. They fight constantly about how to price the wines. Marco says he keeps prices low to give great wine for fair prices to the common people. Giancarlo says they have to make money, because they both work so hard they deserve to be profitable."

"Who wins?" I asked.

"No one. They have had that argument every month for the last 20 years and the prices have never changed," he said.

"That's why we travel all around the country to find unknown, undervalued, but great wines so we can charge these prices. I am their consultant. I was always very knowledgeable about wine and have educated them over the last few years on these trips," he added.

"Did they become wine gurus along the way?" I inquired.

"Marco has, but Giancarlo loves the trips as well. He selects the wine where the winemaker has a beautiful daughter so he can keep coming back there. He has been married quite a few times," he added. "It is always a lot of fun for all of us. This place is our lives."

On return visits, Paolo would open bottles of wine just for us, to show us the best of different regions (Tuscany, Piedmont, Umbria), different grapes, (Nebbiolo, Sangiovese), and different wine types (Amarone, Barolo, Montepulciano). His enthusiasm and emotion were contagious. We always made it worthwhile for them by buying a bottle or two to take home.

Paolo didn't do this just for us. He did it any time a group of attractive young women sat down at a table. Then it was impossible to get his attention. He was the center of every girls' night out.

Over our time in Rome we met a number of other wonderful and quirky members of this crazy club. We became friends with Diego, Paolo, Marco, Giancarlo and Lara. They invited us to their Christmas Eve party, where music blasted and everyone danced. They served free Prosecco to all of their friends there. Our son Ryan had joined us for Christmas week in Rome, and he was astonished that we had all of these Roman friends. The evening ended when they turned the lights off and we all sang "Roma, Roma, Roma," the Rome soccer team's official song, with only a sea of cigarette lighters illuminating the room. Ryan used his iPhone to video it all. He was speechless.

They invited us again to their New Year's Eve party, where we danced in conga lines out one door, through the street, in the other door, around the bar and out the first door, again and again. We closed out the evening with "Roma, Roma, Roma."

That night we told Marco that we would write an article about his amazing place for a major American newspaper to make him and his bar famous. He asked us not to. We asked why. Marco responded that if it attracted a lot of new customers, there wouldn't be enough room for his friends. He just couldn't allow that. We took a series of photographs with all of us together. It was fun, but actually very emotional. They had made us feel like family.

We hated to leave the place when we had to leave for Paris. It was where we had become "true Romans."

ROMA, THE PALIMPSEST

B efore we left for Europe, I took a graduate course at the University of Pennsylvania on Rome. I thought it was a good idea to prepare me for our journey and begin my education. It was offered by the classics department. The course, "Visions of Rome in Art, Literature and Cinema," was fascinating. It was based on the premise that Rome the city was the ultimate palimpsest. This word comes from the ancient practice of using a stylus and a wax tablet or a lamb- or goatskin parchment to communicate a message and then scraping it clean to be used again. This process was a metaphor for the history of Rome itself.

Rome has over 2,000 years of history visible in one place. The tablet that is Rome was first ancient Rome, the city of Augustus, Marcus Aurelius, Caesar, the Roman Republic and the Roman Empire. It was the Colosseum, the Pantheon, the Roman Forum and the Baths of Caracalla.

Then Rome was the early medieval city that was sacked in the fifth and sixth centuries, conquered by the Visigoths, Vandals, Ostrogoths and Lombards. From there, it became the capital of the Papal States. It was under the direct sovereign rule of the popes from the eighth century until 1870. That was the time of the Roman Renaissance and Baroque Rome and when the major churches were built: the Basilica of St. John Lateran, St. Peter's Basilica, the Church of the Gesù and Santa Maria Maggiore, as well as the Piazza Navona, the Trevi Fountain and the Spanish Steps. As the popes attracted and commissioned great artists to decorate these great churches and town squares, the work of Michelangelo, Raphael, Bernini,

Borromini and Caravaggio made Rome the center of the world of Western art.

The next phase was the period of unification and the founding of the Kingdom of Italy. The National Monument of Victor Emmanuel II was added as a tribute to the united Italy's first king.

You can stand at the Piazza Venezia and by turning slowly in a circle, you would make a 2,000-year journey back and forth through history: Trajan's Forum, Trajan's Column and Trajan's Market from the second century; the Victor Emmanuel monument from 1911; the Baroque Palazzo Doria Pamphilj, and the Renaissance Gesù church.

All these eras coexist as you travel around Rome today — sometimes in the same building like the Pantheon, which was built by Augustus and was remade into a Catholic church by the popes. Two thousand years of history on the same tablet: Rome itself is indeed a palimpsest.

CAMERAS IN EUROPE

N o trip to the top European capitals can be complete without a significant collection of photographs. A number of years ago I bought a top of the line Nikon digital camera with a wide selection of lenses. Telephoto, fisheye, portrait, wide-angle, close-up, I bought them all. They were accompanied by flashes, multi-battery power packs and other accessories in a very large and very heavy case. Our children were all three-sport athletes in high school, and capturing those moments seemed worth the expense. I was often the school photographer with the tripod on the sidelines of their football and lacrosse games. I had a big bag of lenses and tried to change them quickly for the one that was appropriate for the action at hand. The 2x telephoto was the one that seemed to get the most use. That is the one you see sports photographers, kneeling in the end zone, using at professional football games. It is awkward to maneuver and requires a monopod extension, a one-leg tripod, to hold up the heavy camera.

I thought this setup would be great for our trip until Lisa told me otherwise. She explained she wasn't going to carry the 16-pound bag of lenses and accessories daily through the streets of Rome, Paris and Barcelona. It just wasn't happening. I needed a new plan.

We then both discovered that the world had changed significantly in the last few years with the continuous improvement of the quality of lenses in smartphones. Where had we been? My iPhone 6 has a 12-megapixel lens with a f/2.2 aperture. That is as good as my Nikon D300. And my iPhone is dated. Even so, it can take panoramic photos that capture a 360-degree view of your subject. My Nikon can't do that. And cellphone camera technology advances dramatically every single year. Now, all of the major cellphone suppliers — Apple iPhone, Samsung Galaxy, Google Pixel — are comparable to traditional expensive digital cameras. Apple introduced the iPhone 8 and X, which leapfrogged my iPhone 6, but my existing iPhone was a pretty amazing touring partner. It was the perfect camera for Monet's enormous semicircular "Water Lilies," which fills two rooms at the Musée de l'Orangerie in Paris. Or the continuous photo of the entire interior of the Colosseum in Rome. Or the glorious panorama of the sun flooding through the stained-glass windows of Sainte-Chapelle in Paris, saturating the room in waves of blue and green.

The iPhone also has a 1080p HD video recording capacity. My Nikon doesn't have that, either. It was perfect for capturing the exciting color-drenched "Magic Fountain" symphony- accompanied show in Barcelona, or for adding time-lapse photography of sunsets on the Barcelona beach, slow-motion, and more. Great stuff.

But the wide range of Nikon lenses, how did I solve that? Third parties now sell attachment lenses for cellphones at reasonable prices. I found quite a number of suitable alternatives; Olloclip and bitplay, and the now-discontinued ExoLens, were just a few. The leader, Moment, offers a 2x telephoto with a 60-mm. focal length, a wide-angle lens, a macro for close ups, and a super fisheye lens that has a 170-degree field of view for photographing expansive vistas. They are all attached via a battery photo case that replaced my existing case and connected by Bluetooth. The lenses are very small and lightweight, attach easily and can be swapped quickly. This was great. My whole camera setup could now fit into my pocket. I could take all of it everywhere.

Nothing escaped my new camera. No church, protest march, gallery painting, lunch, Airbnb interior, late night cocktail hour. And to top it all off, my iPhone software collected all of the photos I took, and using a feature called Memories, assembled them into sets of video collages, added titles, and listed the location of the photos with the help of Google Maps and GPS. The software also added a choice of music to accompany them. I could select "epic" for the Colosseum in Rome, "uplifting" for the view of Florence from Brunelleschi's cathedral dome, "sentimental" for the Venice gondola ride, "happy" for the beach at Barcelona, or just plain "dreamy." This was perfect. It even arranged all of the photos by location as well as by the major sites we had visited, and created collections of St. Peter's Basilica, the Roman Forum, the Louvre, Notre-Dame and the Seville April Fair.

Editing tools are powerful as well. There is a quick-fix feature and wide ranges of effects to lighten and darken, increase contrast, make colors warmer and cooler, and increase saturation. There is even a software slider adjustment for things like exposure, contrast and saturation that allows you to find precisely the right setting.

There are a couple of important techniques that can add a lot to your photography. The first is not to focus only on images you can find in a tour book or brochure. You can start with that, but also take a more creative approach. Don't just take a photo of a famous painting, take a photo of a small, interesting part of the painting. Zoom in on a section. Capture the actual brushstrokes or a fascinating detail. At major buildings and churches, look at interesting architectural elements. Find little details in the design of a statue, or changes in how lighting affects the ceiling of a church or pours through the stained-glass windows — things that make each photo personal, unique and different from what you can find in guidebooks. Also remember that the average Roman or Parisian citizen is often the reason you love the city. Capture them. Capture old streets, alleyways, tiny restaurants, cafés, and laundry drying on clotheslines, which gives a city its color.

Another important element is to do your editing at the end of every day. Do you need to lighten it, make it warmer, or increase the color saturation? It is so easy to take up to a hundred photos a day, and if you don't edit them that day, you will never be able to keep up. Also, remember to be aggressive in deleting photos that aren't excellent. You will never miss them.

Eight thousand five hundred photos later, we decided we had made excellent choices. Cellphone camera, small interchangeable lenses, the software and editing features embedded in your phone. Just remember to learn how to use all of your phone's software before you begin your trip so you can get the most out of it.

It's true. You can leave your "real" camera behind and not miss a thing. We were liberated. We watched and laughed as we saw husband and wife teams lugging their big expensive Nikon and Canon cameras, photographer and pack mule, grumbling and dragging. And my camera pack-mule was set free. Hallelujah for both of us.

ROMA'S MAGNIFICENT
MUSEUMS

Most visitors' shortlist for exploring Rome includes St. Peter's Basilica, the Vatican Museums, the Sistine Chapel, the Roman Forum, the Colosseum, Trajan's Forum, Palatine Hill, the Spanish Steps, Trevi Fountain, the Pantheon, the Piazza Navona and the Piazza Campo de' Fiori. That is a long shortlist, very comprehensive — and potentially overwhelming. That list would give you a great glimpse of every significant period in Rome's history. It would also keep you strolling in the warm Roman sunshine. This agenda would, however, cause you to miss many of the most important works of art of each period. Those works are in Rome's incredible museums: the Capitoline Museum, the Galleria Borghese, the Galleria Doria Pamphilj and the Barberini Palace.

Nothing can compare to the Colosseum for the grandeur that was ancient Rome. But at the top of the smallest but most famous of the Seven Hills of Rome stands the beautiful Capitoline Museum, where you can experience many of ancient Rome's significant artworks. Capitoline Hill was known as "the head of the world" in ancient times. In the 16th century, after the Sack of Rome, its reconstruction was commissioned by Pope Paul III and designed by Michelangelo with a vision to restore it to its original elegance. As you climb the long grand staircase up the hill, walk between the two magnificent knights and their horses that crown the staircase, and enter the Piazza del Campidoglio, the experience is breathtaking. A copy of the enormous bronze equestrian statue of Marcus Aurelius dominates its center. With the elegant Palazzo Senatorio, Palazzo dei Conservatori and Palazzo Nuovo on three sides, you fully appreciate why it took 100 years to complete. These last two buildings house one of the greatest collections of classical art.

Here are the bronze "She Wolf," the mother of Rome and its icon, and magnificent classical statues such as the "Capitoline Venus," the "Dying Gladiator" and the "Drunken Faun" and the original equestrian statue of Marcus Aurelius. The museum also includes a number of great paintings such as Caravaggio's "The Fortune Teller" and "John the Baptist (Youth With a Ram)."

The Galleria Borghese is set at the far edge of the wonderful, pine tree-filled Villa Borghese gardens. It houses a magnificent 20-room collection of High Renaissance, Counter-Reformation and Baroque sculptures and paintings. The five Bernini rooms contain a number of his secular sculptures, including his masterpieces "David," "Apollo and Daphne," "The Rape of Proserpina" and "Aeneas, Anchises and Ascanius." These are breathtaking sculptures and are among his greatest works; their energy, movement and emotion are incredible. Walk around them multiple times to truly appreciate them. Explore the details in the metamorphosis of Daphne from nymph to laurel bush. You will understand why Bernini is mentioned with Michelangelo and Florence's Donatello as one of the three greatest sculptors of all time.

The Caravaggio rooms contain a wonderful collection of his work including "David With the Head of Goliath" and "Saint Jerome Writing." There is a remarkable collection of the works of Raphael, including "The Deposition" and "Lady with a Unicorn." There are equally magnificent works by Titian, including "Sacred and Profane Love." Bellini, Veronese, Rubens and Canova are represented here as well. It's an incredible place that displays the breadth, depth and magnificence of art.

The Galleria Doria Pamphilj holds a wonderful collection of paintings and sculpture. Sculptures include Bernini's bust of Pope Innocent X. Paintings including Caravaggio's "Rest on the Flight

Into Egypt," Velázquez's magnificent "Portrait of Pope Innocent X," Titian's "Salome," Tintoretto's "Portrait of a Young Gentleman" and Raphael's "Portrait of Andrea Navagero and Agostino Beazzano" adorn the walls. Another wonderful gallery.

The National Gallery of Ancient Art in the Barberini Palace is also excellent. It contains Raphael's masterpiece "La Fornarina" and great works by Titian and Tintoretto. But it is the magnificent ceiling painting by Pietro da Cortona that makes it worth the trip. A sea of magical allegorical figures that represent "the virtues" reigning from the clouds gives a powerful illusion of three-dimensionality and is mesmerizing.

Finally, the Ara Pacis (Altar of Peace) Museum is also extraordinary. It was built in the year 9 B.C. to honor Augustus for the peace he brought the Roman world after 20 years of civil war. This monumental altar was rebuilt from fragments in the early 20th century. The carvings on the sides of the altar tell a fascinating story of Augustus and ancient Rome.

THE ART IS IN THE CHURCHES

S t. Peter's tops everyone's shortlist of must-see attractions in Rome. But Rome has over 800 other churches. The Michelin green guide singles out 20 for its highest ratings, two or three stars. It recommends or highly recommends visiting all 20. Who knew? Each of these churches has its own fascinating stories, and many are architectural wonders as well. What drove this collection of amazing churches? The popes and the Roman Catholic Church. They attracted and commissioned the greatest artists of the High Renaissance and early Baroque periods to create magnetic and majestic attractions for the Catholic faithful in Western Europe. These churches were built and then decorated with the greatest sculptures and paintings in Europe, by artists including Michelangelo, Borromini, Leonardo da Vinci, Bernini, Raphael, Caravaggio, Bramante and Pozzo. They all brought their respective art to a grandeur never seen before, and influenced every artist after them.

Visiting these top 20 churches posed both a wonderful opportunity and a challenge as well. There were just so many different approaches to organizing these visits. The first approach was to just to stop in during our many walks around Rome. That is actually what we did. But once we knew much more about them, there appeared three other possible approaches that could weave them all together.

One way could be to cluster them around a tour of the four major original basilicas of Rome: St. Peter's Basilica, the Basilica of

St. Paul Outside the Walls, the Basilica of St. John Lateran and the Basilica of Santa Maria Maggiore. These churches were breathtaking architectural wonders when they were built and remain so today.

St. Peter's and St. Paul Outside the Walls — equally vast and magnificent, with 80 columns and a gold and white coffered ceiling — were designated by Pope Boniface VIII in 1300 as central to the first Catholic Jubilee. The Jubilee was the event that brought the Catholic faithful from all over Europe to visit Rome to receive pardons for their sins. Each pilgrim was required to make 15 visits to each of the basilicas, which held the relics of the two saints, Peter and Paul. In subsequent Jubilees in 1350 and 1375, St. John Lateran and Santa Maria Maggiore were added to this religious journey. The new objective was to visit all four churches in 24 hours for a remission of your sins and a universal pardon. This came to be called the Holy Door Tour because only one special door was opened during official Jubilee years. By 1825, the Jubilee had attracted 500,000 pilgrims.

A second approach to visiting Rome's churches could be to take a seven-church walk, much like the pilgrims during the later Counter-Reformation period, beginning in the late 16th century. This tour added the Minor Basilica of St. Lawrence Outside the Walls, the Basilica of the Holy Cross in Jerusalem and the Sanctuary of Our Lady of Divine Love. In all of these Jubilees and pilgrimages, the objectives of the popes and the Catholic Church were to design, build and decorate such awe-inspiring churches to draw the maximum crowds and, with them, the maximum contributions to all seven churches from pilgrims seeking their plenary indulgence.

Designed by Borromini, St. John Lateran, with its sweeping Baroque architecture, was the original papal palace, basilica and baptistery. Santa Maria Maggiore, with its extraordinary interior of two rows of columns, gold coffered ceilings and the remarkable fifth-century mosaics featuring Abraham, Jacob, Moses and Joshua, is beyond compare. The jaw-dropping design of these churches became the talk of Europe and increased the turnout with every successive Jubilee. In 1450, the crowds were so large that 200 people were trampled to death in an accident crossing the Sant'Angelo Bridge.

The final approach to organizing the church visits would be to seek out the artwork of the High Renaissance and early Baroque periods. The artists whom the popes engaged to decorate these churches were among the greatest in the history of Western art. They included the architects and sculptors Bernini and Borromini, the architect, painter and sculptor Michelangelo, and the painters Caravaggio and Raphael. The art in the churches of Rome is so remarkable that curators of the world's greatest museums would be envious. The extraordinary interiors of High Renaissance, Mannerist and Baroque domes, with their ribbings, window patterns, frescoes and orgies of Baroque paintings, are works of art in themselves.

St. Peter's Basilica is the masterpiece of this collection of great architects and artists. Construction took 120 years and spanned the lives of 20 popes and 10 architects. It was begun by Bramante and finished by Bernini. In 1547, Pope Paul III engaged Michelangelo, then 72, as chief architect. He designed its magnificent dome. Decades later, Bernini built St. Peter's Square with its wonderful colonnade surrounded by statues as well as one of the fountains in the courtyard entrance.

The interior of the basilica contains Michelangelo's sculpted masterpiece the "Pieta." The farewell moment between Jesus and Mary is a calm and transcendent experience. Bernini designed and built the spectacular bronze and gold 95-foot-high Baldachin, the canopy towering above St. Peter's tomb and enveloping the pope's high altar. Bernini also designed the Chair of St. Peter, another elaborate work sculpted in bronze and decorated in ivory, and the Urban VIII and Alexander VII monuments. Borromini added the gates to the Blessed Sacrament Chapel.

Michelangelo created one of his greatest works of art in 34 Old Testament frescoes on the ceiling of the Sistine Chapel. Individual panels, like the famous "Creation of Adam," are great masterworks on their own. Twenty years later, he completed the chapel with another enormous work that fills the back wall of the altar: "The Last Judgment." It is a powerful vision of the end of the world as Christ returns to judge mankind, a sea of muscular naked figures climbing to heaven and falling to the underworld.

Nearby, in the Picture Gallery, are many of the greatest works of Leonardo da Vinci, Raphael and Caravaggio. And in the Vatican Museums we find the extraordinary Raphael Rooms, which include his "Transfiguration" and the magnificent "School of Athens," which pairs the Athenian philosophers with the faces of his contemporary artists. The greatest artists of the High Renaissance and Baroque periods created many of their most powerful works all around Vatican City and the largest basilica in the world.

As we explore Rome further, we find Michelangelo's "Moses" in the San Pietro Vincoli Church and his "Christ the Redeemer" in the Santa Maria Sopra Minerva Church. Another church, Santa Maria della Vittoria, contains Bernini's breathtakingly beautiful and emotionally moving marble statue "The Ecstasy of St. Theresa." And in a mystical experience outside Santa Maria Sopra Minerva, we are greeted by the famous Bernini "Elephant and Obelisk." As for Borromini, he was the architect behind San Carlo alle Quattro Fontane, Sant'Andrea della Valle and Sant'Agnese in Agone churches.

Caravaggio decorated the Cerasi Chapel at the Piazza del Popolo with his famous works, "The Conversion of St. Paul" and "The Crucifixion of St. Peter." He revolutionized painting with his breakthrough in heightened chiaroscuro, or dramatic illumination, in his use of light and darkness, and his use of vermillion and Venetian red. He influenced countless followers, including Rubens, Rembrandt and Vermeer.

Raphael painted the dome's mosaic and Bernini sculpted the carvings that decorate the tombs of Agostino and Sigismondo Chigi with green marble sculptures of Daniel, the lion, the angel and the winged skeleton.

In San Luigi dei Francesi, we find Caravaggio's splendid works, "St. Matthew and the Angel," "The Calling of Saint Matthew" and "The Martyrdom of St. Matthew."

Some of the most incredible works of art are painted directly on churches' ceilings. Andrea Pozzo set new rules for the use of perspective in painting in his extraordinary trompe l'oeil on the ceiling of Sant'Ignazio Loyola. It's a fresco that creates a three-dimensional illusion that the church is 10 stories high and the painting stretches limitlessly up into the heavens. It is photographically realistic imagery. We came back often to see it, the illusion was so captivating.

Another amazing church ceiling is at the Church of the Gesù, the main Jesuit church in Rome, where the artist Giovanni Battista Gaulli, known as "Il Baciccia," painted the famous Baciccia frescoes. "Triumph in the Name of Jesus" uses the trompe l'oeil technique to create the illusion of a continuum between the sculptures of Antonio Raggi that encircle the ceiling and Gaulli's own work. It is impossible to determine where one begins and the other ends. Another dynamic three-dimensional perspective.

The art in Rome's churches exceeded our wildest imagination. St. Peter's Basilica, the Sistine Chapel, the Vatican Museums and the Picture Gallery left us culturally and emotionally exhausted. Many other churches so intrigued us that we returned to see Bernini and Caravaggio again and again. When friends came to town and asked us what most surprised us in our visit to Rome, we brought them to some of these lesser-known churches like Sant'Ignazio Loyola and the Church of the Gesù and they too were astonished. Beyond the Vatican, they also didn't know the art is in the churches.

TOUR GUIDES

I n Europe, we found that most tour guides were knowledgeable
and intelligent. They cared about their country and its history
and culture, and genuinely wanted you to gain a certain amount of
information during your visit.

Our concern was that unless a particular historic or religious site
threatened to overwhelm us, we wanted to learn about it ourselves
and thereby get a deeper understanding. So we decided to go cold
turkey on tour guides. It worked for us with a few exceptions.

The Colosseum and the other Roman ruins qualified as
overwhelming. So did the Vatican. You could get lost in the Roman
ruins for at least a day, and at the Vatican for a week. You wouldn't
even be sure you had seen the most significant works. We needed
a guide for each. The rest of Rome we could do ourselves with the
assistance of our Michelin green guide.

Our guide, Rosa Militano, recommended by a friend of ours,
came equipped with a couple of invaluable books as her assistants.
These books place today's monuments in their ancient context so
you can better understand what you are seeing. If you go without
a guide and without the books, ruins can be reduced to a field of
stones that you can't in your wildest imagination reconstruct as
ancient Rome.

Books the tour guides use include "Rome Reconstructed," "Rome
Then and Now in Overlay" and "Rome Past and Present: A Guide
to the Monumental Center of Ancient Rome with Reconstruction
of the Monuments." Some show what you are actually looking at
in all of its disorganized glory and use plastic overlays to show

what it must have looked like many hundreds of years ago. With the before-and-after approach, you say out loud, "Who could ever have imagined that? It doesn't look anything like that. Where is the Sacred Way? Is that the Temple of Saturn? The Temple of Castor and Pollux? I give up."

The before-and-after overlays are particularly useful at the Colosseum. Your first impression is, what a gigantic crazy empire of jagged rough stones. These illustrative books, accompanied by an effective tour guide's narration, make you actually understand what an amazing feat its creation and daily operation must have been.

Vatican City was another story. The Vatican museums by themselves could take a week to explore. Packed with tourists as they normally are, maybe even two to three weeks. But when an aggressive Roman guide has you in tow, barging in and dragging you through the crowds, it is an entirely different experience. Scusi. Scusi. Scusi.

With someone who does this professionally day in and day out, you can discover shortcuts and be forcefully steered to the extraordinary works of art. And throughout the Vatican museums, the Raphael Rooms, the Picture Gallery, the Sistine Chapel and St. Peter's Basilica, there are countless works that qualify. Michelangelo, Leonardo da Vinci, Bernini, Raphael, Caravaggio, Bramante. All of the masters of the High Renaissance and Baroque periods of Rome. And too difficult to navigate without an assertive, knowledgeable Italian tour guide.

Beyond Rome, any adventure in Europe without the pleasure of exploring one or more great wine regions would be a shame. We selected the Brunello di Montalcino vineyards of Tuscany and the Châteauneuf-du-Pape vineyards of the Rhône region of France. They were two excellent choices. Our terrific local guides, Silvia Romano and Sophie Bergeron, whom we found online, negotiated entry into hard-to-visit properties where we enjoyed excellent restaurants and tastings. They drove us around challenging mountain roads, backing up on a cliff's edge to allow other cars to pass. They were always fun and funny as well. A must do!

For the majority of your adventures, be your own guide. But for a vital few, select your guide well and it will be well worth it.

Restaurants in Roma

Most visitors are attracted to Rome by the incredible breadth of ancient, High Renaissance and Baroque Roman sights. When you arrive, however, you become equally astonished by the wide variety and high quality of the restaurants. We have always avoided the restaurant recommendations in travel books. By the time they are published, the restaurants' profiles may have changed considerably. The exceptions are the Michelin red guides, which are updated every year. Should we start there?

There are relatively few Michelin stars among the restaurants of Rome – just 21 over all in 2017. Compare that to Tokyo's 304 stars, Paris's 134, New York's 99 and London's 79 stars. But countless cozy, warm, friendly, family-run Roman trattorias are of extraordinary quality. Each one is quirky, unique and tries to make you feel special. How would one determine the best? The internet. Never just stop in.

Of the newspaper reviews, the most comprehensive are in the U.K. papers. The Guardian and The Telegraph tend to have the widest English-language coverage of Rome. Among magazine websites, Condé Nast Traveler and Bon Appetit may be the best. There are also different websites focused specifically on restaurants in the top European cities. For Rome they include Revealed Rome, Romewise and The Culture Trip, and these are also kept up to date. (Trip Advisor is skewed by its large number of young people and student users and isn't especially useful for moderately sophisticated travelers.) We searched all of these sources to find where several agreed on a restaurant.

The key to eating in Rome is to eat like a Roman. The other keys are to always make a reservation and to get there before the Romans do. If the guidebooks tell you to arrive when the Romans commonly do, around 1:30 or 2 for lunch and 8 for dinner, ignore them. Arrive when the restaurant opens for lunch, which is usually at 12, and at 7 o'clock for dinner. Get there first. Pick out the best table. Get to know your waiter. Ask him or her for all of their favorites and their customers' favorites. Order sparking water and wine the second you arrive. And order before too many others do.

We always made lunch our big meal. We took on average 2½ hours over a long, relaxing stay. We didn't rush. No one rushed us. That's just being Roman. Afterward, we would begin our sightseeing for the remainder of the afternoon. Walk it off. No breakfast before lunch, just coffee or tea. No dinner after, unless that was the only meal the restaurant served, and then we would substitute it for lunch.

The most frequent complaints on restaurant-review websites are about being turned away without reservations, or waiting too long to get your waiter's attention, too long to get the menu, too long to get served. Also, that the staff was rushed and not paying sufficient attention, and the restaurant was out of their specials. You avoid all this by always making a reservation and getting there first. We never had an issue with any restaurant over our three months in Rome. In every restaurant we returned to, they remembered us because we got to know them before they were too busy. And we behaved like locals, not tourists.

We researched the best restaurants in every section of Rome and took into account the sightseeing we planned in that area of town. We walked to all of them. Over 10 weeks in Rome, we visited more than 30 restaurants and returned to nine of them multiple times. The reviews we read often even told us their individual specialties.

Early on, we would order a pasta dish and a main course at each trattoria. But this became too much food at some of them. When we returned, we would split each course between us. All of Rome's restaurants were very supportive of this approach, unlike in the United States.

The classic Roman pasta dishes were the core of the start of every menu. Amatriciana (or gnocchi all'Amatriciana) with its fresh tomato sauce, strips of crispy guanciale (pork cheek), Pecorino Romano, white wine, chili pepper and possibly garlic or onions is a great one. Cacio e Pepe with its thin tonnarelli or vermicelli pasta tossed with finely grated Pecorino Romano and coarsely ground black pepper is simple and wonderful, and finally Carbonara with its hot tonnarelli woven into a creamy mixture of egg yolks, Parmigiano Reggiano, Pecorino Romano, black pepper and crispy cubes of guanciale was excellent as well. Peas, leeks and mushrooms are also sometimes added. You might think you wouldn't want one of the big three every day, but nothing could be further from the truth. Everyone in Rome does. These pasta dishes are Rome.

What was our favorite restaurant? That is a very difficult question. We had nine favorites. How could we have nine favorites? Well, we were in Rome, the home of the simple friendly, welcoming trattoria. We ate at each of our favorites at least three times. Lisa went out of her way to make friends with the waiters and waitresses in each one, and they, in turn, treated us special. In every restaurant, every single day, we ate one of the big three pastas. In addition, we shared every dish at every meal.

Casa Bleve was a few short blocks from our place, around the corner from the Pantheon. High, stained-glass ceiling, comfortably spaced tables, soft light. Great wine and fabulous food. Try the carpaccio or tartare of the catch of the day, or the baked cod.

At Armando al Pantheon all of the classic Roman pastas are extraordinary, but pay the extra for the truffles option. It was unbelievable. Also try their unique Roman soups, especially the artichoke soup. The saltimbocca and the lamb chops were delicious. The restaurant is just 200 meters from the Pantheon's porch. We had a favorite waiter who steered us to specials not on the menu and gave us the quiet table in the corner.

Osteria del Sostegno is a few blocks past the Pantheon off a side street and down a little alleyway. Half of the tables are inside and half are outside. Great pastas. Outstanding chicken cacciatore. Friendly and efficient staff. Another favorite table outside, and a special waitress who spoiled us.

Osteria dell'Ingegno is directly across from the old ruins of Hadrian's Temple, which is now the Italian stock exchange. Great ambience, lighting, location and music. The pastas are excellent and their fresh seafood is even better. Loved the sea bass. Always captured their only table on the porch.

Dal Cavalier Gino is across from the Palazzo Montecitorio (Chamber of Deputies) down a little alleyway. It is as Roman as you can get. Cash only. As in many of these restaurants, many of the waiters speak very little English. You need to learn to read all of the menus in Italian, and do your best to order in Italian. Our favorite waiter would always tease Lisa in Italian. She had no idea what he said, but she would laugh anyway. Great saltimbocca and rabbit.

Trastevere's best trattoria is Da Enzo. It is a little hole-in-the-wall and always crowded, cramped and loud. Its excellent, fun, high-energy staff make up for it. All of the food is incredible. Everyone's favorite dish is the burrata d'Andria. The tiramisu is to lust after.

Hostaria Romana has the best antipasto in Rome: assorted cheeses, cured meats, marinated sardines, sautéed eggplant, mushrooms and baby artichokes. The restaurant is on a small side street off the Piazza Barberini. In the lower-level room, they let you write on the walls with colored markers. Everyone does. The pasta is excellent and the seafood is amazing. The waiters are fun and funny. When we said we would like to split our main course, a seafood dish, they brought Lisa the complete deboned fish and brought me the skeleton they had deftly removed. They then put fresh ground pepper on my skeleton. We all laughed hysterically.

Hostaria Romanesca is right on the square at the Campo de' Fiori. Fresh pastas made by the owner's mother every day. Great inexpensive wine. Great seafood bought daily from Rome's famous fish market right around the corner. Try the swordfish in the spicy tomato artichoke sauce.

And you must try Pianostrada, run by a woman, her two daughters and her best friend. It you get a chance, sit at the bar and watch them cook. Unique dishes and great tastes. The staff are all characters and are friendly and funny. The family liked us and sneaked us in even when they were fully booked. The food is to die for.

We never had a bad meal in Rome. Some restaurants were crowded. In some, the service was slower when they were busy. The food, however, was always very good and often excellent. Getting there early, asking for wine and sparkling water, and ordering before the crowd arrived, we were always relaxed, happy and in control. And we never got tired of simple fresh pasta, fresh seafood, broiled lamb or chicken, and simple local white Italian wines. And good company. Perfect.

MOTOR SCOOTERS IN ROMA

Rome is one of the most romantic cities in the world. We think about Audrey Hepburn, the elegant secret princess, and Gregory Peck, the handsome, sly American reporter gleefully flying around the city on their Vespa in the romantic 1953 film "Roman Holiday." Marcello Mastroianni and the Swedish blond bombshell Anita Ekberg and the classic beauty Anouk Aimée, tearing around Rome in his convertible in "La Dolce Vita" in 1960. They created an everlasting fantasy about fast times and love in this crazy city.

Today, personal transportation in Rome is a challenge. Italy has the most passenger vehicles per capita in Western Europe. In this sprawling metropolis, with some central areas little changed in a hundred years, there are very few places to park. The subway system is the least developed in Europe because the city tries to avoid disturbing ancient ruins underground. There is a passable bus network, but it doesn't always keep to a schedule. So many people choose to drive.

Parking is a real challenge, even though the cars are small: The Smart car, Mini Cooper, Fiat 500, Hyundai Accent and Honda Fit are all popular, as is the Twizy, a tiny electric Renault. With most of the cars so compact, the average Roman believes you can park anywhere on the sides of the narrow Rome roads and alleyways at a myriad different angles and directions — traditional, facing in, facing out, facing the wrong way on a one-way street, in the middle of roundabouts, on the sidewalk, and sometimes just in the middle of the road. Anywhere you choose, it seems. There seem to be no clear rules on what is in or out of bounds for these Italian drivers.

The answer for many people is the simple scooter. Well, it is actually not so simple. There is a potpourri of alternatives that range from what look like electric bikes to powerful motorcycles. The majority are somewhere in the middle. The popular Italian Vespa has sold more than 16 million with scores of models over 70 years. There are also the Italian Moto Guzzi, Benelli, Beta, Garelli, Piaggio and the famous Ducati. The Japanese are well represented by Suzuki, Kawasaki and Honda, the French by Peugeot and the Germans with BMW. Scooters are cheap to run — many of them get 100 miles per gallon — and you can park them virtually anywhere. And people do.

The riders include grandmothers who get off and walk with canes, shop owners, businessmen in suits, members of Parliament, young women of every description and teenagers. Fourteen-year-olds are allowed to ride 50cc models. Driving styles vary wildly, and there often seem to be no rules of the road. Scooters travel between stopped cars, down pedestrian-only streets, the opposite way down one-way streets and on sidewalks, ignoring traffic lights and generally going wherever the drivers think they want to go at that moment. If you can think it, you can do it. At the morning and evening rush hours, scooters look like an endless pack of locusts and sound like them as well.

Why the fascination of scooters for Romans? They are sometimes their only significant possession, so they become a passion. Romans' apartments are often small and sparse. Many are unhappy with their jobs. Many Romans hate life's rules and pride themselves on disobeying or ignoring them. Both men and women carry a spare helmet on the chance they meet someone in a café. Spontaneous romance is Romans' other true passion. At any age.

Scooters are at the core of the Roman psyche, are a true extension of the people themselves. The size of the engine, the sound of the revving and acceleration. The colors. The shape of the bike. The helmet. The random, deliberate or reckless way they drive are all extensions of their personalities. The tens of thousands of scooters in motion become the ids, egos and superegos of the overall population of the city.

After watching this every day, walking down the streets of Rome, crossing and weaving, dodging, jumping, even when we had a green light, I asked Lisa if we could rent one. No way José was her reply. Yeah, I guess.

The sad truth is there is a real downside to all of this crazy behavior, as much fun as it may first appear. Rome is reported to be the most dangerous city in Europe for traffic accidents. Everyone is aware of the risks, but they don't change most people's behavior.

At the Communist Bar, we asked how our friend Diego makes it home safely on his scooter after drinking wine for a few hours with us. He told us, "no problem." Another friend, Paolo, told us that Diego lived only four blocks away, and sometimes got only a block or two before he crashed. Oh, so that sums up the story of motor scooters in Rome.

Bars in Roma

Well, you already know our favorite bar in Rome was the Communist Bar. There are quite a number of other great bars in Rome. Bars for great wines. Bars for great appetizers. Bars for tourists. Bars for locals. Bars for people watching. Bars for everything. Lisa found that bars were the perfect way to weave a network of friends across Europe. If you are prepared to talk to everyone at every adjacent table through numerous rounds of drinks, you can meet a significant number of people in a reasonably short time.

We met families from New Zealand, hedge fund managers from the U.K., young couples from our own Philadelphia, art professors from Annapolis, Md., retired couples from Germany, groups of touring Australian rugby players, kids who turned out had gone to college with our kids, college professors of our friends' kids, visiting business executives, U.N. officials, and government agency heads. Name a part of the world or a demographic segment, and Lisa had intertwined them into her global network of new friends. It was almost like when our youngest child was 8 years old and he told my mom he was so happy he had 67 friends. Lisa now had more.

One of our favorite outdoor wine bars was the Cul de Sac, located on a busy square, the Piazza di Pasquino. It offers a wonderful menu of interesting cheeses, pâtés, cured meats and inexpensive wines on communal wooden tables. It was packed by 11 a.m. and stayed busy all day. When we found a spot, we would sit and converse and interact for hours with the eclectic crowd swirling around us, and this location, the square, connects travelers returning from St.

Peter's and those traveling to and from the Campo de' Fiori and Piazza Navona.

Bar del Fico was also off the Piazza Navona. It is an inexpensive shabby-chic bistro that caters to chain-smoking locals playing chess outdoors on its many rickety tables. Second-hand vintage furniture throughout, always packed, high energy, great music. We got to know many of the locals there.

We would alternate these bars with the sophisticated bars on the other side of Rome near the Spanish Steps. The Stravinskij Bar in the chic Hotel de Russie is wonderful for people watching and engaging in cosmopolitan conversation. In its gorgeous outdoor garden, nothing less than a Champagne will do. The tables are filled with Rome's beautiful people. The bar in the Hassler hotel at the summit of the Spanish Steps has a timeless elegance with its dark wood, red leather upholstery and gilded mirrors, and is filled with an equally interesting and sophisticated international clientele. The Imago bar and restaurant on the hotel's sixth floor has an extraordinary panoramic view of Rome. Watch the sun set on Capitoline Hill, the Pantheon, the Victor Emmanuel monument and the Piazza Navona.

Caffè Canova-Tadolini is great for a glass of wine in the original studio workshop of the neoclassical sculptor Antonio Canova. It is a chic museum-cafe where you are nestled among his original sculpture models in every nook and cranny.

Salotto 42 is a hip, noisy bar across from Hadrian's Temple. Freni e Frizioni is good for young crowds, high energy and free food; the Caffè Perù for noisy fun and a real local appeal; Enoteca il Goccetto a wine lover's heaven, for great antipasto and beautiful people.

The Prohibition-era speakeasy is a big new idea for Rome bars like the Jerry Thomas: secret passwords, no signs, sliding door slots with code names at the mysterious entrances. Bartenders are dressed in outfits from the 1920s. It's always crazy and fun, with wild exotic drinks as well.

Finally, the biggest and most popular dance club in Rome was just down the block from us. Shari Vari Playhouse opened at midnight and stayed crazy until morning. From our balcony, we could hear the patrons going home as the sun was rising. Five floors with different music themes: dance, hip-hop, electronic and more. Cosmopolitan and international. We arrived at 12, danced our way around the place and were out by 1:30 a.m. when it was starting to get really crazy.

Lisa was right. The way to appreciate Rome, actually every European city, is to connect with everyone. Tourists, locals, waiters and bartenders. It is the only way to weave yourself into the fabric of a place. Fit in. Develop a passion to return. Make it your city. Forever.

'The Sack of Roma'

Some people hear the expression "the Sack of Rome" and think of Aug. 24, 410, when the Visigoths led by King Alaric destroyed the city. The event was seen as the major landmark in the fall of the Roman Empire. Rome itself was rebuilt a number of times over the years, but it never again regained the power it had in ancient times.

Today, tourists have Rome in their sights. When we first began our walking tours, we were astonished by the volume of tourists. Rome itself has three million inhabitants, but over the course of the year draws seven million to 10 million tourists. In the peak season, the tourists outnumber the residents. Buses clog all of the major streets. Tour guides, their flags held high on poles, lead thousands of lemmings with headsets and identical hats, following one another down every major street. They can fill smaller streets from side to side in tightly packed human rivers that are often impossible to cross.

Peak attractions like the Trevi Fountain can attract crowds 50 people deep. Tourists climb the steps of some of the churches that surround it just to get a peek. Forget about taking a photo of the fountain that isn't 95 percent filled with people.

It has been said that Europe has become Disneyland for adults. In Rome, that sure seemed true. The proportion of tourists to native Romans must overwhelm the proportion of attacking Visigoths in 410. "The new Sack of Rome." Were we equally guilty?

The same is true of Venice. A city center of 50,000 Venetians, down from 175,000 in 1951, it hosts 20 million tourists every year. Cruise ships clog the canal and blot out the unique and beautiful landmarks. Languages are a multicultural soup of Chinese and English, not Italian.

The same is true in Florence. With 13 million visitors between April and October, tourists also dwarf the 383,000 native inhabitants. Tourists clogging the streets and bridges, and students eating fast food on the steps of churches, leaving behind cups, wrappers and other refuse, make the journey a challenge.

This sack of Rome can be seen from multiple perspectives. Florence is also the home of the elite of the fashion industry — Gucci, Prada and Ferragamo, to name a few. About 16 miles away is the city of Prato. The combination of Florence and Prato was the historical capital of Italy's textile business. Today in Prato there are 4,000 Chinese-run clothing workshops and factories, an official from a local trade group told the BBC. More Chinese factories than Italian factories. According to Reuters, as many as 50,000 Chinese live in the area, up to two-thirds of them illegally. Fires and safety violations are endemic, and many workers log 14-hour days. Between 2001 and 2011, the Italian textile industry saw its revenue and Italian workforce fall by half, the leader of a business group said. Shoe uppers and half-completed handbags are shipped in from China and India and assembled in Italy. Then they are stamped, "Made in Italy."

But factory owners seeking cheap labor are not the only culprits. The influx of tourists has robbed Rome, Florence and Venice of some of their magic and their sense of historical grandeur. Rather than linger to take in the beauty, too many travelers just check sights off their lists and rush on to the next city.

AIRBNB

After selecting the major European cities where we were
interested in staying, choosing the Airbnbs as our home bases
was our most important early decision. It gave us a feeling of security
that we would be anchored for large parts of our trip.

We bought a map of each of our key cities, Rome, Paris and
Barcelona. We used the Michelin green guides to mark every
important museum, statue, ruin, church, fountain, opera house
and other significant site on these maps. In Rome, we identified 80
significant items, in Paris 40 and in Barcelona 35. That was the big
difference between most couples' two-week vacations in a city and
our approach. We wanted to really know everything about each
city, to investigate every important site and to steep ourselves in its
culture by following the city through the ages.

We triangulated these sites on each city map to find the center
of all of the locations we had highlighted. That approximate center
was where we investigated apartments most aggressively. In Rome,
it turned out to be next to the Pantheon. In Paris, it was the Sixth
Arrondissement, St.-Germain-des-Prés, right off Boulevard St.-
Germain. In Barcelona, it was on the harbor in Port Vell, a short
block from the back corner of the Gothic Quarter. We intended to
walk almost everywhere. No car. No taxis. No metros.

This was our first involvement with Airbnb. We believed the
selection would be very important because we would be staying in
those three cities for three months each. We ended up scheduling
an additional three cities with no previous experience selecting or
experiencing Airbnbs: Florence, Siena and Seville. It was a bit of a

risk, scheduling all six without any lessons learned from our first encounter. We ended up with one superb location, two acceptable ones, two troublesome ones and one disaster.

A few words to the wise. First, never, ever believe the photos on their websites. That is the best the places will ever look, the illusions of great lighting and photography. There is zero chance you will have a pleasant surprise, except if the surprise is that it looks like the photo. Second, read every comment from previous renters. Those comments are the most valuable information on the Airbnb site. They will alert you to many of the surprises you will actually be faced with.

Third, remember that in Europe every floor number is actually one floor higher than in the U.S. What they call the first floor is really the second floor, the second is the third and so forth. Many of these buildings are five and six floors tall. In many of these older buildings with high ceilings, the steps from floor to floor are a very long walk, even if the floors are marble. There's a reason these apartments get less expensive the higher you go. These can be very, very, very long climbs. Always try to get an apartment with an elevator, but remember, most of these have been added after the building was built and are very small. Most struggle to fit two adults and their groceries. In some cases, you even have to send your largest pieces of luggage up by themselves. If a building does not have an elevator, never select a room above the third floor, and ideally choose the second floor. This is especially important if you intend to leave and return two or more times a day. And if your attraction to the apartment is the photos of the beautiful rooftop view of the city, don't fall for it. The daily walk to your apartment could be a nightmare.

In examining the comments on the website, the most important thing to note is the responsiveness of the owner or manager to problems with the place. And, trust me, there will be problems. Problems with the washer, dishwasher, stove, heat, air-conditioner, toilet, Wi-Fi, and with unusual light bulbs that have burned out and are hard to replace.

Views can be appealing, but comfort and reliability are more so. Remember that you will be spending most of your time outdoors. Location in the city is always the most important factor.

Finally, read the terms and conditions regarding canceling your reservation. The cancellation fees can be severe even with significant notice. In addition, be careful about corresponding terms and conditions that may allow the host to cancel your reservation. Airbnb has an arbitration process but it tends to favor the owner. Every lesson we learned here, we learned the hard way.

The guideline we settled on was don't rent an Airbnb unless you will be in one location for at least a week. That is the threshold that determines whether you will need a washing machine to avoid high laundry fees and a kitchen so you can do a little cooking with local ingredients. For the shorter stays, a hotel was always more predictable and drama-free. A little more expensive but a safe refuge. And better odds for an elevator.

Firenze: Birthplace of the Renaissance

In the 15th century, Florence became "la culla del Rinascimento," the cradle of the Renaissance. Between 1300 and 1600, it was the sponsor of the humanist movement in Europe and the rebirth of the scholarship of the original Greek and Roman texts in history, literature, civics and philosophy. It was the home of the Platonic Academy, Neo-Platonism and the translation of the ancient Greek works of Plato and Aristotle into Latin.

This cultural rebirth was also the foundation and inspiration for the greatest collection of artists and sculptors in the history of the world at that time: Donatello, da Vinci, Michelangelo, Raphael, Botticelli, Brunelleschi, Giotto and Ghiberti. All except Raphael were born and raised in the Florentine Republic. These artists used science to create breakthroughs in art and architecture in the ways they employed perspective, geometry, foreshortening (shortening lines to create the illusion of depth), sfumato (blurring outlines to create the illusion of three-dimensionality), and chiaroscuro (strong contrast between light and dark to create the illusion of depth). In addition, two Florence scholars wrote the first books on architecture: Andrea Palladio wrote "The Four Books of Architecture," and Leon Battista Alberti wrote "On the Subject of Building." They remained "the reference" on Western architecture for decades.

Florence became the Athens of the Middle Ages and the early Renaissance. It counted among its leading thinkers and poets: Dante Alighieri ("The Divine Comedy"), Petrarch ("Songbook"),

Niccolo Machiavelli ("The Prince"), Marsilio Ficino ("Platonic Theology"), Pico della Mirandola ("Oration on the Dignity of Man") and Poliziano ("Manto"). For over one hundred years, it was the intellectual and artistic center of the Western world.

Florence was also the center of medieval European trade and finance and one of the wealthiest cities of that era. The Medici family financed everyone from the English kings to the papacy. They also commissioned the great works of Michelangelo, Leonardo da Vinci and Botticelli. They built some of the greatest churches in Europe including the Basilica Santa Maria del Fiore (the Florence Cathedral) and its associated Florence Baptistery, and the churches of San Lorenzo and Santa Maria Novella to display that art.

The exquisite beauty of Florence, its churches, museums and some of the world's greatest works of art, lured us like a siren's song. Donatello's "David," Botticelli's "Birth of Venus," Michelangelo's "David" and the Florence Cathedral's magical dome all drew us in. And we were going to see them close up after the tourist season had wound down. We couldn't wait. It has been said that Florence hasn't changed in nearly five hundred years. The Athens of the Middle Ages has been preserved in amber for all time.

When we stepped off the train in Florence in November, we were greeted by a blast of Arctic air. We walked up the platform into the station building and were freezing even though we had ski coats on. We quickly stuffed our luggage into the trunk of a taxi and jumped into the back seat. It was a short ride to our Airbnb through pitch-dark one-way streets.

We got out in the black night and pushed the bell for our fifth-floor apartment. After a short wait, a young woman came to the door and told us the owner was unavailable due to a broken foot and she would escort us to our place. We climbed up the tiny stairway, floor after floor. We remembered that fifth floor really means sixth floor in Europe. We could barely drag our luggage up these 12 sets of very narrow steps in the freezing cold stairwell. By the time we reached the apartment, sweat was dripping off our noses. The young woman opened the door and showed us in. It was essentially one big room with a double bed in one corner, a small kitchen table, a set of matching, tired living room chairs, and the kitchen in another corner of the room. She showed us around, explained how the dishwasher and washing machine worked and handed us the renter's manual, which included instructions for the various appliances and a list of recommended restaurants.

The place had the décor of a grandmother's or great aunt's apartment, with a musty smell, funny old curtains, an old tired rug, and assorted knickknacks on shelves and tables everywhere. We had a brief discussion with the woman and asked if it was always this cold. She explained it was the coldest day of the year. A cold front had come down from northern Europe, but even so, it was the coldest day she could remember. But I looked out the back window and saw the most glorious view of the brightly lit dome of the Florence Cathedral. It looked so close I could almost reach out and touch it. It was an extraordinary church, glowing in the dark night. It was a heavenly sight. This view would make this rooftop apartment worth it, despite the horrible walk up the steps to reach our eagle's nest.

We left the small apartment, walked a few blocks to a restaurant, had a light meal and returned for the night. The temperature in the apartment had dropped significantly. We checked on the unusual heating system in the back corner of the kitchen. The contraption looked as if it was built in the 1940s: twisting pipes, valves, switches, old fashioned dials and meters, and a big tank that we assumed held water. The thermometer said it was 40 degrees Fahrenheit. Jesus. We riffled through the rental manual but remained clueless about how it worked. We finally called the owner's number in the back of the book.

Switching back and forth between English and rapid-fire Italian, the owner told us that we must have had the heat too high and it had shut itself down. We said we hadn't touched anything. She told us all of the dials we needed to turn down to allow the pressure to build up, and then how to flip other switches to jump-start the gas. Then, at a certain pressure level, we needed to normalize the pressure again for the night. We told her that we weren't mechanics or engineers and were afraid we would blow ourselves up, and we asked her to come over. She said her foot was broken and her husband wasn't home. She would send him in the morning. We said we would be dead from the cold by then. After a very heated exchange, we gave up and went to bed, fully dressed and in our ski coats, gloves and hats. So this is Airbnb. A nightmare.

When I woke up, I felt like I was a boy scout camping in a tent in the dead of a snowy winter. We were freezing. We called around and finally found a hotel room. We packed our bags and left. We knew from last evening's telephone exchange this was never going to work out. But we were still alive. We would negotiate later the penalties for leaving early.

After checking into the hotel, we found the gym we had identified two blocks away, and we changed and went to work out. And by the time we had returned and showered, we felt back in the game and our enthusiasm for the glorious city of Florence had been restored.

We were magnetically drawn to three of the buildings in the Piazza del Duomo: the Cattedrale di Santa Maria del Fiore, the Florence Cathedral; Giotto's Campanile, or bell tower; and the Battistero di San Giovanni, the Florence Baptistery. They were almost beyond description. Right out of a dream. Four of the greatest architects and sculptors of the Renaissance had a hand in their design: Brunelleschi, Giotto, Ghiberti and Donatello. These three magical structures are both an integrated mystical whole and three individual works of art. They shimmer in a divine harmony of polychromatic wonder. Their exteriors are united in a grand geometric pattern of white marble from Carrara, green marble from Prato and red marble from Siena. Even after visiting the Vatican, we were astonished by these architectural works of art. It was as though we had entered another world.

The octagonal Baptistery was constructed between 1059 and 1128. It was the first of the buildings to use the geometrically patterned colored marble. It is beautiful. However, it is the Baptistery's three sets of bronze doors and their relief sculptures of biblical stories that make this building a unique work of art. Lorenzo Ghiberti beat Brunelleschi and Donatello to win the commission to build two sets of these doors, and the job took him and his workshop 27 years to complete. The first set had 28 panels depicting the life of Christ from the New Testament. The second had 10 panels depicting scenes from the Old Testament. Michelangelo referred to these doors as fit to be the Gates of Paradise.

The interior walls are clad in dark green and white marble with inlaid geometric patterns. The mosaic marble pavement with its complex zodiac imagery is fascinating. But it is the magnificent Byzantine-style mosaic dome ceiling with its iconic figures resting on a gold background that takes your breath away. Five rising concentric rings depict stories of the Last Judgment and the Book of Genesis.

Giotto's free-standing Campanile is equally majestic. The five-stage tower has polygonal buttresses at each corner and is 278 feet tall. It holds seven glorious bells that enchant visitors and residents alike. Its design employs the same geometric marble patterns as the Baptistery and the Cathedral. Each of the five levels is decorated with hexagonal panels depicting either biblical or Neo-Platonic messages, along with statues by Donatello and other great sculptors woven into the niches on each side. Climbing its 414 steps to the top gives you a scenic panorama of Florence and the surrounding countryside.

It is the Florence Cathedral, with its astonishing dome engineered by Filippo Brunelleschi, that is the centerpiece of this sacred memorial to the Renaissance. Construction of the building took more than 140 years and was completed in 1434, but the dome required an additional two years. It was the first octagonal dome built without a temporary wooden supporting frame.

At the time, the Florence Cathedral was one of the largest buildings in the Christian world. It occupies close to 90,000 square feet and is over 500 feet long and 300 feet wide at the crossing, and the dome rises 375 feet high. The exterior walls are done in the same polychromatic marble as the Baptistery and the Bell Tower. Together, Ghiberti and Brunelleschi worked on the cathedral for 18 years.

The interior of the 147-foot-wide dome is covered with a mosaic representation of the Last Judgment and a series of religious frescoes. With 44 stained-glass windows by Donatello and Ghiberti, the Gothic interior is vast and seemingly empty. That is because most of its fascinating interior decorations, such as the magnificent cantorial pulpits (singing galleries for the choristers), have been moved for safekeeping and are on display in the Opera del Duomo Museum next door. The work in this museum is amazing in itself.

The remainder of our six days in Florence was filled with other extraordinary museums and churches. But the Piazza del Duomo and these three breathtaking buildings lured us back every day, sometimes more than once. At the cafés in the piazza, we sat at window tables, sipping rich espresso or big, bold Tuscan wines, staring at these magnificent sights, mesmerized by the geometric multicolored marble design. It changed with the hour, depending on how the sunlight or the violet-tinted evening spotlights affected it. It was almost like the series of Monet paintings of Rouen Cathedral that change with the light, and we were in the painting. We too were crystalized in the amber of Florence.

We found the four major museums of Florence astonishing as well, as they contain most of the great works of art of the early Renaissance period. The Uffizi Gallery has da Vinci's lyrical "Annunciation," expressive "Adoration of the Magi" and "The Baptism of Christ;" Botticelli's "Madonna of the Magnificat," the spiritual and allegorical "Birth of Venus" and the dazzling "Spring;" Michelangelo's powerful and complex "Holy Family (Doni Tondo);" and quite a number of splendid Raphaels.

The Bargello holds Donatello's bronze masterpiece "David" and imposing "Saint George," and a number of sculptures by Michelangelo including the so-called drunken "Bacchus," the powerful "Brutus," the unfinished "David Apollo" and the great "Tondo Pitti."

The Galleria dell'Accademia contains Michelangelo's masterpiece, the 17-foot-tall marble biblical hero "David," as well as his four huge unfinished "Prisoners" and "Saint Matthew."

Donatello's and Michelangelo's "Davids" are a study in contrasts. Donatello's bronze "David" stands with his left foot on Goliath's head, bearing the giant's sword. He has an almost feminine pose and a slim, graceful, adolescent form. Michelangelo's "David" may be the most monumental marble nude since antiquity. It has a heroic scale and a superhuman beauty. His neck and torso muscles are straining, and his veins seem to bulge from beneath his skin. Both were designed to represent the spirit of Florence.

The Pitti Palace, the mansion of the Medicis, is an architectural joy in itself. It is filled with the art of Raphael, including the brilliant colors of "Woman With a Veil," the gentle "Madonna of the Grand Duke" and the subtle "Madonna della Seggiola," and a number of works of Titian, including his fascinating "Portrait of a Gentleman."

But the wonderful churches of Florence hold much of its great art as well. The Basilica of San Lorenzo was both designed and decorated by Brunelleschi. The interior includes two extraordinary pulpits and an equally extraordinary sacristy, whose bronze doors contain 40 figures of holy martyrs and apostles. At the adjacent Medici Chapels, Michelangelo created his powerful statues depicting day, night, dawn and dusk.

Santa Maria Novella, whose exterior is also decorated in the famous Florentine green and white marble pattern, is filled with dazzling frescoes. Santa Croce has the harmonious Donatello "Annunciation."

Over time, the popes lured these great artists to Rome. Michelangelo, da Vinci, Botticelli and Raphael were all attracted to the Vatican by large commissions to do some of their greatest work in the period of the High Renaissance for Leo X, Julius II and others. But their achievements in Florence set them among the greatest artists of all time.

Their work is woven into the fabric of Florence forever. Never had so many extraordinary architects, sculptors and painters taken root almost at once. They created one of the most important cities in the history of Western Europe. And traveling there was like being transported to the 15th century. Crystalized in amber forever.

SIENA

It was a short trip by taxi, just 3½ miles, from the Stazione Ferroviaria di Siena, the train station in Siena. But the winding ride with its switchbacks through one-way streets gave us a fascinating glimpse of the wonderful little hilly Gothic town. In most of this medieval village, cars are not permitted, so we had to weave this way and that to get to our central destination.

We were to meet Nazarene, mother of the Airbnb owner, Luisa, at the Palazzo Tolomei. It is a privately owned 13th-century mansion just off a square in town that our taxi driver would know. When we arrived we were surprised to find a tall column in the center of the square, with a bronze statue of Romulus and Remus being suckled by the she-wolf atop the column. It turned out this represents the symbolic birth of the city when Senius, son of Remus, arrived from Rome.

Nazarene was waiting for us, a smiling, smartly dressed woman in her early 70s. Her gray hair was pulled back tightly into a bun. She seemed excited to see us and welcomed us with a big handshake. She then waved her hand for us to follow.

We walked downhill along a broad cobblestone street, Via Banchi di Sopra, weaving through a sea of pedestrians. Everyone walked everywhere in Siena. We dragged our wheelie suitcases bobbing on the cobblestones. After a number of blocks, we turned into a narrow street and came to a large wooden door. It was the only home on the street. We walked up a flight of stairs, and Nazarene welcomed us into a well-lit, spacious apartment.

Nazarene showed Lisa how to operate the appliances and where things were. She also explained that Luisa was sorry she couldn't meet us, but she was taking her daughter to a Lady Gaga concert. She shook our hands once again and told us she hoped we would have a wonderful time in her town. Everyone loves Siena.

We didn't even unpack, we were so excited to explore this wonderful old village. Lisa and I bounced out the front door, turned left at that main street and continued down the hill to try to find the Piazza del Campo, the town's fan-shaped central square. The street curved to our right, and a series of tunnels led off from it and headed down into the piazza. We took the second tunnel, and when we emerged we were drenched in the warm Siena sun. It was glorious.

We were magically transported back to the 14th century. On the far, "flat" side of the fan of the piazza is the Palazzo Pubblico, the picturesque Gothic town hall, which is also a museum. Next to it is the Torre del Mangia, a slender tower. The rest of the fan is encircled by tall, medieval brick buildings and a series of restaurants and bars with outdoor seating under canopies. These were filled with people laughing and talking in small and large groups, one of them singing football songs. What a wonderful cosmic energy the piazza generated.

We took two seats in the outdoor bar where the group singing football songs was sitting. Their laughter and horseplay were contagious. What a fun place this was. Lisa and I ordered two glasses of Prosecco and bathed in the sun and song. What a great introduction to this great city.

After a while, we paid our bill and decided to head back to our apartment. We needed to get unpacked, find our maps and guidebooks, and build a plan to explore the city. We returned through the tunnel where we had entered the piazza, turned right and headed back up the hill. Nothing looked familiar. Every building was that same camel color. Every roof had the same look of burnt toast. We walked until we reached the Palazzo Tolemei. Too far. Returned to the tunnel. Too far. Then we realized we never had the address of our place. It wasn't listed on the Airbnb site. Nazarene never gave it to us. We never asked. We had the scary realization that we didn't know where we lived. After three more anxious trips up and down the hill, we began to get really nervous. Every building in Siena looked alike to us. Every street did. We were starting to panic.

We returned to the bar where the football fans had been singing. They still were. We needed a plan. First we ordered a bottle of Prosecco and a plate of cheese. How do we find out where we live? We didn't even have Nazarene's number. Just chill with the Prosecco. I know, call Luisa. I still had her number from when I talked to her from the U.S. After a few tries, I finally reached her at the concert. She gave us the address, 4 Via di Calzoleria. Thank God. We plugged it into our iPhone Google Maps software. Nothing. Our street didn't exist in the software. Maybe because it's the only house on the street. Panic again. Called Luisa again. Sorry. She slowly explained to us to walk up Via Banchi di Sopra until we reached the Bar Pasticceria Nannini and then turn right. It is right there. How could we get so lost in such a small area? Silly but true. We headed home.

In the morning, we went back to the Palazzo Pubblico. As far back as the 12th century Siena had been an independent republic. Its merchants and bankers were famous throughout Europe. As a city-state, it was a threat to Florence. From the mid-13th century to the mid-14th century was its heyday and when most of the great buildings and palaces were built. Then, between 1348 and 1350, it was decimated by the Black Plague. The epidemic reduced the city's population by 27,000, or two-thirds. The city never fully recovered economically or politically.

The Palazzo Pubblico is a showcase for the Sienese School of painting. Two rooms there, the Sala del Mappamondo and the Sala della Pace, are graced with the works of some of the greatest Sienese artists: Ambrogio Lorenzetti, Simone Martini and Duccio di Buoninsegna. A Lorenzetti work, "The Effects of Good and Bad Government," is a fascinating illustration of the city's thoughts on the proper administration of the city-state. The tower next door provides a superb panoramic view of the entire city.

The Cathedral Precinct is a short walk away. Besides the Duomo, the cathedral itself, it includes the Museo dell'Opera and the Battistero San Giovanni, all on the Piazza del Duomo.

The Duomo has an extraordinary cross-section of Sienese art. The floor of the cathedral is composed of 56 marble panels created by 40 artists depicting figures from mythology and scenes from the Old Testament. The marble pulpit depicts the life of Christ in seven panels. It is supported by nine marble and granite columns. In the Libreria Piccolomni, a series of 10 panels of brilliantly colored frescoes depict the life of Pope Pius II.

The museum contains Duccio's masterpiece "Maesta," or "Majesty," among its great works, a large altarpiece with scenes from the childhood of Christ. In the Battistero, or baptistery, is an extraordinary basin decorated with bronze panels that was created by a series of great artists including Ghiberti and Donatello. It is a mesmerizing work that depicts a series of episodes from the life of John the Baptist.

Although the architecture, sculpture and painting in Siena are wonderful, it's the people who make it a special place. In the restaurants, the wine bars, the pizzerias, everyone is open and friendly. This welcoming, inclusive style is just part of the fabric of this wonderful medieval village.

When Lisa and I sat alone at the bar of Grand Hotel Continental, the bartender wandered over and educated us about the Palio di Siena, the raucous medieval-style horse race held twice each summer. In the Piazza del Campo, tens of thousands of spectators watch from bleacher seats, windows and balconies that ring the piazza. Ten riders from the city's 17 contrade, or neighborhoods, compete each July 2 and Aug. 16. The bartender insisted that we return for it and handed us a brochure.

She explained that the day begins with a two-hour pageant, the Corteo Storico, with over 600 people in historical costumes, ox-drawn chariots, drummers and ancient-looking floats. Then the race involves three laps around a third-of-a-mile track with tight turns. The competition is very intense, and more than 50 horses have died since 1970.

In the restaurant Enoteca i Terzi, the owner educated us about the highlights of Tuscan food. He gave us a tour of his wine cellars and explained the differences in grapes and tastes of the major Tuscan wines. He then helped us select a delightful meal of artichoke soufflé, risotto with asparagus and rabbit with olives.

It was similar at the small, cozy Taverna di Cecco. The owner seated us and told us about the Tuscan specialties. The chef came out to meet us and we had another great meal, this time truffle risotto, osso buco and a great Montalcino wine the owner suggested.

It was the same at the wonderful Osteria le Logge. Surrounded by shelves of wine bottles, books and antiques, we had another great meal of pasta, truffles and pigeon. We later were given a tour of their enormous wine cellar.

The bartender at the Untubo jazz club took us through the history of the ward-centric contrada culture, which originated in medieval times. Each contrada has its own identity and mascot, such as a snail, porcupine or a she-wolf. This is the basis of the competition of the Palio di Siena horse race.

What a wonderful, inclusive culture Siena has. No wonder it has such a fabulous reputation among travelers. Another Italian city frozen in amber since the 14th century. We agreed we had to return for the crazy horse race one summer.

Venezia: The Mysterious Island City

I t's called "the City of Water," "City of Bridges," "the Floating City" and "the City of Canals." Venice is a mysterious collection of 118 small islands located on the Venetian Lagoon, between the mouths of the Po and Piave Rivers, separated by countless canals and connected by 400 bridges. It has been ranked the most beautiful city in the world.

The buildings of Venice are constructed on closely spaced wooden piles made from the trunks of alder trees, a wood noted for its water resistance. Submerged in oxygen-poor conditions, they don't decay as rapidly as on the surface. Most of these piers are still intact after centuries in the water. The foundations of Venetian homes rest on plates of limestone on top of the piles and are built of brick or stone. Hence the name, "the Floating City."

Venice was a major financial and maritime power during the Middle Ages and Renaissance. It was also Western Europe's first international financial center. It was the third major city, after Florence and Rome, that was an important home to the Renaissance artists. "The Venetian School" included the glorious masters Bellini, Giorgione, Titian, Tintoretto and Veronese. It taught a style of painting characterized by deep, rich colors, an emphasis on patterns and surfaces, and a strong interest in the effects of light. These artists created an entirely new style of painting that was filled with warm reds, golds and greens. Their figures were arranged in three-dimensional space. Yet another city that evolved into a world-famous museum.

Our timing was right for Venice. In a city troubled by the problems caused by an excessive number of tourists in peak periods and choked by oversize cruise ships crowding close to its banks, we would arrive in the off season and truly enjoy ourselves alone in this paradise.

We exited the fast train from Rome at Santa Lucia, the Venice train station, incredibly excited to see this mythical city. It was the second week of December. The tourist crowds were long gone. The terminal was fairly empty, so we really thought we might have the city to ourselves. As the main glass doors opened when we approached, we were shocked. The city was blanketed in a sea of swirling fog. We should have realized that Venice, being in the center of a large body of water, the Venetian Lagoon right off the Adriatic Sea, might be surrounded by fog in the winter. But we never saw it coming.

We pulled our luggage down a long ramp to the west end of the Grand Canal. In the thick fog, it was difficult to see directional signs, never mind where the vaporetti, or water taxis, would moor. Navigating their unusual numbering scheme and their destinations was tough enough in the bright sunlight. As the vaporetto appeared in the distance, our fellow passengers were quickly boarding. We passed the ticket machines and entered the empty travel office. We had to get this right.

We bought two tickets for unlimited travel for the week. We knew we were heading to the San Zaccaria station, where our hotel was, which was the Route 3 vaporetto on our map, but we instead took the Route 1 boat, the slow boat. We wanted to spend time crawling through this incredible city in the swirling soup of fog.

As soon as we boarded, the sweat from our rush to the boat began freezing on our pink faces. We didn't realize how cold it was. We had ski coats on but were still shivering slightly as the boat surged away from the dock. Maybe the slow boat wasn't such a good idea after all.

I hung onto a railing to try to see all of the sights through the fog. I saw ghosts of those classical and unique Venetian Gothic, Renaissance and Baroque homes breaking through the fog and then just as quickly disappearing in the distance. Three hundred years of architectural evolution and refinement spinning in and out of focus. I strained to see anything except the landing docks coming in and out of view as we dropped off and picked up additional passengers. Then, out of nowhere, something enormous approached from above. It swallowed us up. As we were directly beneath it, I finally recognized it: the solid stone Rialto Bridge. We really were in Venice.

The trip was cold but beautiful and peaceful in the thick fog. Then I started to panic. I thought I would recognize the Piazza San Marco and the Doge's Palace, but at every vaporetto stop we couldn't see a thing until we briefly docked – and then we'd be whisked away. How would we even know we had arrived? We stopped for a moment at the Gallerie dell'Accademia art museum, and then it disappeared in the thick fog. Was that the ninth stop or the 10th? Where did we need to get off? I should have done a better job getting specific directions but I had thought the hotel would be easy to find. Another stop where I didn't recognize the name, and then another. Finally, I could see the San Marco stop coming into view. We rushed to the side of the vaporetto and jumped off. But we still couldn't see anything through the fog. We just followed those who had exited before us, down a wide pedestrian road called Riva degli Schiavoni. Our wheelies tipped and jumped down the cobblestones. In the distance, we saw the outline of the Basilica di San Marco fade in and out. We crossed a bridge and another bridge. Five minutes later, our waterfront hotel came into view. We were safe.

Our first question to the check-in clerk was how often this blanket of fog affects Venice. Only for December, she said matter-of-factly.

The next morning after working out in the hotel gym and a light breakfast, we retraced our steps in the floating, swirling fog back to the Piazza San Marco. We found the square eerily empty. The fog added an interesting dimension to our photography. Mysterious. The Basilica di San Marco peeked out of the fog and then disappeared, again and again. The four glorious domes that graced its enormous roof, and the four bronze horses topping the large central doorway arch, fading in and out of view. The fog would lift briefly to reveal the carvings above that central arch as well as the mosaics at the top of the four adjacent arches. The same thing happened at the Doge's Palace and the tall bell tower as its spire and golden weathervane appeared and disappeared. We were witnessing a perspective of Venice that few tourists ever saw.

The basilica was our first destination. As we entered, we were surprised to be encircled by a packed congregation of both sitting and standing worshipers. We were entranced by the sounds of its glorious pipe organ and the waves of singing by its choir. We had happened upon the Sunday High Mass. In our constant immersion in different landscapes, panoramas, artistic visions and the urban symphony of sounds, we sometimes lost track of the day of the week. Actually pretty often. But this was a wonderful surprise.

An enormous convergence of worshipers and tourists snaked their way around the basilica. We tried to remain unobtrusive as we took in the glistening Byzantine mosaics that lined the walls and the ceiling. The first level depicts the saints, the middle the apostles and the inside of the domes, the Creator. The area above the atrium is the Last Judgment. As we reached the front, we marveled at the Pala d'Oro, the golden altarpiece commissioned from Constantinople. A masterpiece of the goldsmith's craft, gleaming with pearls, garnets, emeralds, sapphires and rubies. This basilica is a wonderful confluence of Byzantine, Gothic and High Renaissance styles. We bathed in the glorious uplifting sounds of the Mass, and when it ended and the parishioners exited, we toured this wonderful church again to admire a truly incredible work of art in itself.

We toured the equally amazing Palazzo Ducale, the Doge's Palace, now a museum of the city's greatest artists. Everything is elegant: the Chamber of the Four Doors, the College Chamber, the Chamber of the Council of Ten, the Council Chamber. These rooms and their entire ceilings are filled with the work of Bellini, Veronese, Tintoretto, Titian and others. Tintoretto's "Paradise" takes up an entire wall of the Council Chamber, and Veronese's "Apotheosis of Venice" covers its entire ceiling, to name just two examples.

The Gallerie dell'Accademia covers the entire history of Venetian art. Bellini was instrumental in bringing the Renaissance style to Venice, and his "Virgin in Glory With Saints" and "Procession in Piazza San Marco" are exhibited here, as are Giorgione's "The Tempest," Titian's "Pietà," and Veronese's "Mystical Marriage of St. Catherine" and his controversial "Feast in the House of Levi." This wonderful gallery requires at least half a day to absorb these breathtaking works.

As in Rome, an extraordinary amount of Venice's great art is in the churches. The front altar of I Frari is adorned by Titian's magnificent "Assumption of the Virgin." It is a breathtaking 22-by-12-foot icon of the Venetian style that draws your eye from the apostles on earth depicted in brilliant reds and lifts your gaze to Mary in a glowing red robe. Her arms extend skyward as she is carried into the heavens on a cloud surrounded by cherubs bathed in golden light. Titian then lifts your eyes farther into the heavens, where Mary is greeted by God and a winged angel bearing a crown. A glowing masterpiece of Renaissance art.

San Rocco has a series of wonderful Tintorettos decorating its walls and ceilings, and San Zaccaria's stunning interior is covered in paintings including Bellinis. The Scuola di San Giorgio degli Schiavoni has the extraordinary and passionate "Cycle of St. George" series by Carpaccio, and San Zanipolo, Venice's greatest Gothic church, has a number of wondrous Veroneses.

Like Florence, Venice in the Middle Ages and the Renaissance was a city of extraordinary artists supported by commissions from a powerful community of trading and commerce. And along with Florence and Rome, Venice became one of the most important cities for art in Europe.

In a change in approach from our other European cities, we decided to make dinner our big meal in Venice. We needed more time during the day to be able to complete our agenda. There was only one problem. If navigating the 400 bridges, countless canals every block or two, and Venice's maze of tiny nameless streets was difficult in the daytime, at night in the fog it was nearly impossible. We would go up and down the same street countless times trying to find the side street we needed on our iPhone Google map. The Google map was inaccurate about these tiny streets most of the time. We often went down a street to find that it ended at a canal and no bridge was nearby. Sometimes while staring at my iPhone and blindly following the Google map voice directions in a foggy, dark Venice alleyway, I almost walked directly into the canal. Eventually we got better at it but never good. That said, there is a wonderful, wide assortment of excellent seafood restaurants all over the city. The restaurant staff are very, very friendly and attentive, and all our choices proved excellent.

But one cannot leave Venice without a ride in a gondola. Touristy, yes. Corny and a cliché, yes. But you have to do it. The view from the gondola traveling under the bridges and through the back canals of Venice is unforgettable. We were surprised that nearly all Venetian homes, no matter how small, have a back door right above the canal waterline as a second entrance. This is the best way to get a great, intimate close-up feel for this mysterious island city. You can't miss it.

In the end, we were sad to leave the swirling fog-filled city of canals that we had almost all to ourselves.

PARIS, AN INTRODUCTION

P aris is known by many names. The City of Lights. The City of Art. The City of Love, the most romantic city in the world. Couples arm-in-arm drifting along the edge of Les Quais, eyes connecting, locking, then aimlessly scanning the Seine, Ile de la Cité, Notre-Dame and the Louvre and returning to connect once again. Speaking in soft, seductive French, the language of love.

The largest city in Europe in the Middle Ages, Paris gave birth to early Gothic architecture and the age of cathedrals. It was the center of the Age of Enlightenment and the Age of Reason, and was Western Europe's philosophical heart. Home to Descartes ("Principles of Philosophy": "Cogito ergo sum"), Montesquieu ("The Spirit of the Laws"), Rousseau ("The Social Contract") and Voltaire ("Candide"). Two centuries of philosophers were nourished here. The French Revolution became the foundation of democracy in Western Europe as well. World philosophical leadership continued in Paris with Sartre ("Being and Nothingness"), de Beauvoir ("The Second Sex") and Camus ("The Stranger").

This was all underpinned by the University of Paris, founded in 1150, the second-oldest in Europe (after the University of Bologna). It became the College of Sorbonne in 1257 and has remained a center of European intellectual life for over 800 years. It produced John Calvin ("Institutes of the Christian Religion"), Thomas Aquinas ("Summa Theologica"), Balzac ("The Human Comedy") and Diderot (the "Encylopédie"), among many others. This system, now 13 universities, employs over 300,000 people today.

Paris was also the home of the Impressionist revolution in painting and sculpture. And then the Post-Impressionists, the Expressionists, the Fauvists, the Symbolists and the Cubists. Home to Monet, Renoir, Degas, Manet, Modigliani, Cézanne, Rodin, van Gogh, Dalí, Matisse, Chagall and Picasso. The areas of Montmartre and Montparnasse were centers of the advances in Western art for over one hundred years.

It was the mythical birthplace of multiple generations of men of letters including Hugo ("Les Misérables"), Baudelaire ("The Flowers of Evil"), Proust ("Remembrance of Things Past"), Zola (La Bête Humaine), Dumas ("The Three Musketeers") and Flaubert ("Madame Bovary").

The Lost Generation of the 1920s was nurtured here as well: Hemingway ("The Sun Also Rises"), Fitzgerald ("The Great Gatsby"), T.S. Eliot ("The Waste Land"), Stein and Joyce ("Ulysses"). Writers were drawn from all over Europe and North America to interact in this unique intellectual melting pot with their peers.

Countless attractions bring people to Paris, but above all is its stature as the world's most extraordinary outdoor museum. You can walk its streets forever and your thirst is never quenched. Why is this true? What makes this city so mesmerizing? Who created this?

In 1853, Emperor Napoleon III had the grand vision to rebuild Paris as a modern capital and the greatest city in Europe. He appointed Baron Georges-Eugène Haussmann, Prefect of Seine, to execute his master plan.

The reason the city had to be modernized was that between 1800 and 1850, Paris's population had doubled, to over one million. It had a massive overcrowding problem and its design was still a medieval style of unplanned, narrow winding streets. The streets had confusing layouts and were not efficient for traffic or commerce. They had open gutters carrying raw sewage that were breeding grounds for disease. In 1832, a cholera epidemic in the overcrowded city center killed nearly 20,000 people.

Louis-Napoleon's vision had important political considerations as well. Over the years, Paris had been involved in numerous revolutionary movements. The narrow streets were easy to barricade and difficult for troops to navigate. The new, broad streets would essentially eliminate barricading and provide quick access for troops and, it was hoped, avoid future revolutions.

Haussmann's plan also included the division of Paris into arrondissements and a reorganized road system. This new symmetry laid out the city in a grid. Haussmann built the dozen avenues that radiated from the Arc de Triomphe. He added the transportation infrastructure of the Gare de L'Est and Gare du Nord railway stations.

Haussmann created the uniform neoclassical style of facades for many of the city's buildings, gas lighting for the streets, new aqueducts and a greatly expanded sewer system. Buildings were now allowed to rise five or six stories because of the wide boulevards. By 1878, the sewer system had expanded to 360 miles. New parks were created, like the spacious Bois de Boulogne and the Bois de Vincennes, as well as new monuments. The construction of the magnificent Palais Garnier for the Paris Opera was part of this. Over all, the core of the construction lasted 20 years, and some elements continued for 70 years.

The eclectic Palais Garnier was the "pièce de résistance" of the third wave of Haussmann's plan. The facade has very elaborate multicolored marble friezes, and lavish statuary portraying figures from Greek mythology. The auditorium has a traditional Italian horseshoe shape with seating for 1,979, and the stage is the largest in Europe. The building has a large ceremonial staircase of white marble with a balustrade of green and red marble, which divides into two divergent flights of stairs leading to the Grand Foyer. It has been called the most famous opera house in the world.

Haussmann's overall project destroyed 20,000 buildings and created 30,000 new ones. Sixty percent of the city's buildings were rebuilt or demolished in this "Haussmannization" of Paris. In his memoirs, he called it the gutting of Paris. Haussmann's master project eventually ended up enormously over budget and he had to be fired. Soon after, Napoleon III was defeated in the Franco-Prussian War and went into exile. But their work was done. The most majestic city in Europe was created by 1870. This is the city that largely stands today. A city that is an extraordinary living museum.

It is this grand city that houses the spirits of Paris's past, generation after generation of philosophers, poets, writers, painters, sculptors and fashion designers. They follow you everywhere you go in Paris if you let them. They are your official tour guides from history.

Haussmann's design set aside the ground floor of most every building for the stores and restaurants that we see today lining every city street and allowed Paris to become the gastronomical capital of Europe. There are now as many as 40,000 restaurants. Paris has the largest number of three-star Michelin restaurants in Europe, and total stars awarded, by a lot.

These are some of the elements that give Paris its limitless smells, colors and personality. And the city's enduring design for its buildings, a great many of them still without elevators, was for the affluent to occupy the first and second floors and the less privileged to get the third and fourth floors. We were a third-floor couple.

In what other city in the world would presidents personally direct the establishment of cultural institutions as their legacies? Georges Pompidou left the Centre Pompidou. Valéry Giscard d'Estaing left the Musée D'Orsay. Mitterrand left the Opéra Bastille. Chirac left the Musée de Quai Branly. American presidents never propose anything except their own libraries as remembrances. That is what makes Paris, Paris.

EVERYONE LOVES
IMPRESSIONISM

E veryone loves Impressionism. At least people think they do. If
you ask for their favorite Impressionist artist and painting, they
might say Vincent van Gogh and "The Starry Night." Sorry, he's a
Post-Impressionist. That is a different school of painting. Unless you
were an art history major or took a course on Impressionism at your
local museum, you probably know very little about Impressionism
other than that you just like it.

I love Impressionism. The last course I took in art history was
in middle school. Clearly, I arrived in Paris without a clue about
Impressionism except that I loved Monet's "Water Lilies" when I
saw it at the Museum of Modern Art in Manhattan. Actually, I even
confused Monet and Manet. Also, a dirty little secret of mine is that
I didn't know van Gogh wasn't an Impressionist either. So this trip
to Paris was going to be a great educational experience.

We were very excited about exploring art in Paris. We bought
a one-year pass to the Louvre. Couldn't wait to get there to explore
the Impressionists. We found the Louvre was excellent for Egyptian
antiquities, Oriental antiquities, Greek, Etruscan and Roman
antiquities, Islamic art, the arts of Africa, Asia, Oceania and the
Americas, Italian paintings, Spanish paintings, and northern
European paintings. But not French Impressionism.

The Impressionists are at the Musée d'Orsay. The most
magnificent collection of Impressionism in the world is showcased
there and at the Musée de l'Orangerie and the Musée Marmottan

Monet. Collectively, they tell the story of one of the greatest revolutions in the art world, which put Paris on the map as one of Western civilization's great centers of painting. Visiting these three must be one of your top priorities in Paris.

The Musée d'Orsay is an astounding transformation of the former Gare d'Orsay Beaux Arts railway station. In 20,000 square feet of space on four floors, it houses the largest collection of Impressionist and Post-Impressionist masterpieces in the world. Of their 2,000 works of art, there are 86 Monets, 56 Cézannes, 46 Pissarros, 46 Sisleys, 34 Manets, 24 Gauguins, 19 Seurats and many more of the Impressionists. Inching from one masterpiece to the next was borderline overwhelming. You occasionally had to stop and catch your cultural breath.

Just a short walk across the Seine from the Musée d'Orsay over the magnificent neoclassical Napoleon-era Pont de la Concorde is the Musée de l'Orangerie in the west corner of the Tuileries Garden. Here you will find the most sensational work in Monet's "Water Lilies" series. Eight prodigious water lily murals cover two huge oval rooms from floor to ceiling and end-to-end, with the exception of the entrance doors. Breathtaking. You can sit encircled in this Zen-like experience for hours. It brings you into Monet's world, allowing you to experience the artist's passion as he created the landscaping project that resulted in the water lily ponds. The 250 artworks that followed are now seeded throughout the world. I took pictures of just small sections to examine his attention to detail in this masterpiece. Extraordinary.

The Musée Marmottan Monet borders the Bois de Boulogne in the 16th Arrondissement. It originally was a hunting lodge for the Duke of Valmy. It houses over 300 Impressionist and Post-Impressionist works by Monet, Degas, Manet, Sisley, Pissarro and Renoir. It holds the largest collection of works by Monet in the world. It is much less crowded than the larger museums in the center of the city. That made it a more personal and intimate experience with these amazing works. Included is "Impression Sunrise," the painting whose name is said to have given rise to the overall movement. Be careful, you are not allowed to photograph these works. The photography police take their jobs very seriously here. It is, however, another astounding collection.

Before the Impressionist revolution, the French had imitated the best techniques of the great Italian Renaissance, Mannerist and Baroque painters and the northern European and Spanish painters who followed their styles. The Emperor Napoleon filled the Louvre with these works, first for his own enjoyment and eventually the public's. At the great art institute of Paris, L'École National Supérieure des Beaux-Arts, students were taught what was called "academic painting," imitating the old masters and often replicating their grand religious, mythical or military themes. The École des Beaux-Arts was located in St.-Germain-des-Prés, just across the Seine from the Louvre. This style of painting was the only type that could qualify for the singularly important annual Salon exhibition, where works were selected by those same teachers and like-minded critics who determined what qualified as great art.

In the 1860s, that all changed forever. The Impressionists created a revolution in painting that put Western art on a new trajectory. They were influenced by a series of events that occurred at almost the same moment in time. The first was the rise of the artist Gustave Courbet, who pioneered French Realist painting by emphasizing peasants, laborers and the reality of French country living. Courbet influenced Manet, and Manet, in turn, influenced the other Impressionists with his work.

The second influence was the evolution of scientific thought involving the optical effects of light and their impact on painting. The third was Georges-Eugène Haussmann's dramatic renovation of Paris, which included building the first grand railway stations and knocking down entire neighborhoods to create wide tree-lined boulevards and majestic buildings, parks and gardens.

The next influence may at first glance seem insignificant, but had a major impact: the changes in how paint was created (premixed pigments vs. artist-ground mineral pigments mixed with linseed oil) and stored (from big pigs' bladders in the studio to new portable tin paint tubes). The design of brushes also changed, to a flat head in addition to the existing round ones, and coarse bristles rather than smooth ones made from sables' tails, which changed the artist's brushstrokes dramatically. And at the same time, the new French box easel, or field easel, now allowed portability and painting "en plein air," or outdoors.

Artists were also influenced by the potential threat of photography, but chose their own course rather than compete with it. And finally, the connection of Paris to the rest of the country through the new railway infrastructure allowed artists to easily get to the countryside and the ocean to paint. It was the confluence of all of these factors that was the catalyst for Impressionism.

This new movement was created by a collection of students at the École des Beaux-Arts who influenced one another both at school and after hours at the Guerbois and the other cafés of Montmartre. They included Claude Monet, Pierre-Auguste Renoir, Edgar Degas, Alfred Sisley, Camille Pissarro and others. Their new work was almost universally rejected by the exclusive Salon, but with the help of Manet they created an alternative exhibition, the Salon des Refusés, or Salon of the Rejects. They then held eight Impressionist exhibitions between 1874 and 1886. Over the years, they continued to inspire each other with their new approach to painting. They had very different personalities, economic realities and political views, but they had one thing in common: They wanted to change Western art forever.

They also took an entirely new approach to what would be the subjects of their paintings, and tried to capture a snapshot of a fleeting reality. Although they switched subjects and sometimes even imitated one another's work, each man had a core focus. Degas often concentrated on movement and scenes of fleeting action, like the ballet or the racetrack. Monet was often focused on capturing the light of a constantly changing landscape, the same scene in different light, again and again. Renoir turned to the lives of ordinary people, and on nudes and bathers in later years.

Their styles had a good deal in common: short, thick, visible brushstrokes; colors applied side by side, rather than blended, to make them more vivid; careful attention to natural light and shadows; and the elimination of black in their palettes, with the notable exception of Manet. No one had painted like this before.

Visit the museum bookstores at the beginning (not the end) of your visit to guide your path through their works and instruct you what to look for in these amazing artists. Listen to the audio guide if you have the time and patience. Observe their work up close to see the brushstrokes, and stand back to absorb the impact of their color choices. Maybe even visit the museums twice. These artists changed painting forever.

A great deal of the Impressionists' art gained little acceptance during their lifetimes. A single Paris art dealer, Paul Durand-Ruel, bought a significant number of their works to keep these artists housed and fed through the many lean years. He is said to have bought 5,000 Impressionist paintings, including 1,500 Renoirs, 1,000 Monets and 800 Pissarros. Mary Cassatt, one of the few American Impressionists, introduced Durand-Ruel to gallery owners and wealthy collectors who were friends of her brother Alexander, the president of the Pennsylvania Railroad. Once the Impressionists' work really gained acceptance, it was the Gilded Age in the United States, and this new, fresh, modern art was precisely what these newly wealthy industrialists like Andrew Mellon, Henry Clay Frick and Andrew Carnegie were looking for. Durand-Ruel sold more than 100 Impressionist works to the Philadelphia patent medicine magnate Albert C. Barnes. But it took some time for Europe to recognize these painters' significance in the history of Western art.

I love Impressionism and the dramatic stories behind this uniquely French rebellion in art.

Bread, Cheese and Wine Shops in Paris

P aris is the greatest city in the West for food. Its 141 Michelin stars, by one count, lead every city in Europe and North America, trailing only Tokyo worldwide. But the key to Paris's gastronomical delight is not only its restaurants, bistros and brasseries. Much of the magic belongs to its boulangeries (bakeries), fromageries (cheese shops), caves à vin (wine shops) and patisseries (pastry shops). All Parisians in every arrondissement have their favorites. Actually their favorites near their home, near their office and along their walk to or home from the métro. We all have that mental picture of Parisians scurrying down the boulevard with a baguette or two under their arm or ripping off a bite of a jambon beurre (ham and butter) sandwich while walking.

Only in France, however, has food become a premier area of national pride. Every four years, the French Ministry of Labor organizes and awards the medal of Meilleur Ouvrier de France (MOF), the Best Craftsman of France. It is a unique and very prestigious award. In addition to many of the traditional crafts, there are awards for best bakery, pastrymaking, cheesemonger, chocolatier, butcher and fishmonger. It is a very hard-fought competition. There even was a documentary, "Kings of Pastry," about the MOF pastrymaking rivalry. Medals are awarded at the Sorbonne, followed by a ceremony attended by the president of France at his residence, the Elysée Palace.

We decided that if it was that important to the president of France to recognize the nation's best in food, we would make it that important to us. Using Patricia Wells's famous "Food Lover's Guide to Paris," we began an odyssey to take her descriptions of the best of the best on our expeditions.

Wells used an entire chapter of 30 pages to evaluate the boulangeries across Paris's 20 arrondissements. Thirty pages on bread? We looked up her top three choices, filled her book with sticky notes and began our journey. Lucky for us, all three had stores within walking distance in the Sixth and Seventh Arrondissements: Poilâne, Eric Kayser and Le Pain Quotidien.

The morning we approached Poilâne, we were enveloped by the smell of fresh bread from 30 yards away. The swirling aroma of caramel, hazelnut and spices lured us to the door. We entered to find a number of young women in brown smocks and an older woman sitting at a vintage cash register. We turned and saw a wall of the best bread in Paris, if not the world. It was their masterpiece, the "miche," a five-pound round sourdough with a thick crust engraved with a big P. This gently sour brown bread baked in wood-fired ovens is what made Poilâne famous.

No baguettes for Apollonia Poilâne, the franchise owner and manager. She has run Poilâne since 2002, when she was still a student at Harvard and her parents were killed in a helicopter crash, according to The New York Times. She would carry on the tradition of the first family of bread in France who started their first shop in 1932.

Poilâne herself is now responsible for the 160 people who bake 3 percent of all of the bread for the residents of Paris, Condé Nast Traveler said. Every morning they deliver to the Elysée as well as to 2,500 supermarkets and restaurants.

We carefully selected a loaf as well as a few tartelettes aux pommes — caramelized apples in rich puff pastry that are to die for — and a small bag of buttery shortbread cookies. The miche was glorious, covered with melted cheeses or soft-boiled eggs, or just slathered in rich French butter as our main meal of the day. Wonderful.

Next on our list was Eric Kayser, which offers 50 varieties of bread and pastries, and 25 varieties of croissants. Morning, lunchtime and after work, the lines often go out the door and down the street. There are more than 20 Eric Kayser boutiques in Paris alone, and they have expanded to cities across Europe, the Middle East and Asia as well as New York and Washington.

The experience was very different from Poilâne, but the smells were just as enticing: chocolate, tomato, pumpkin, cranberry, all swirling around. There were wonderful light, crispy, buttery croissants, and crusty baguettes, still warm. And a variety of sandwiches made on those warm baguettes: jambon beurre, of course, but also jambon fromage, fresh tuna with lettuce, tomato, hard boiled eggs and mayonnaise, and chicken with lettuce and Dijon mustard. We became addicted to these sandwiches and had something new each time, even cheating a few times on our lunch-only resolve. Always a treat to visit Eric Kayser.

Finally, we went to Le Pain Quotidien, which had great round, dark rye bread, great baguettes and great sandwiches.

These were all excellent choices. You can see why the boulangerie is a foundation of Paris life. Every Parisian has a favorite shop for every category of bread — boule, chapeau, couronne, fer à cheval, ficelle, fougasse, viennois — and will argue for it enthusiastically. The Concours du Meilleur Croissant au Beurre AOC Charentes Poitou is the fierce competition that determines the best croissant in Paris. The Meilleur Baguette de Paris, equally contested, decides the best baguette, an honor awarded by the mayor of Paris under the criteria of cooking, crumb, taste, smell and appearance. The winner becomes the supplier to the Elysée for the year. In Paris, the boulangerie is integral to its people's way of life.

On to the cheese: cow's milk, goat's milk, sheep's milk. Different aromas, textures, colors, forms and flavors. Countless varieties based on the soil, climate and vegetation variations around France. There are between 150 and 200 major varieties of cheese.

The French consume close to 26 kilos (57 pounds) of cheese per year per person, compared with 15 kilos for the average American. That is 70% more. They actually consume more than anyone in the world. In France, making cheese has become another form of art. One of the main reasons the cheese is so exquisite is that it is often made from raw (unpasteurized) milk. Such cheese is barred by the United States Department of Agriculture if it is aged less than 60 days. These cheeses use natural microbes that may include 24 reproducible types of bacteria. This is what gives them such distinct flavors.

Patricia Wells gave us 20 pages of glorious fromageries in Paris. We made another short list of four within walking distance on the Left Bank and got on our way to another set of aromatic and savory discoveries.

We began with Quatrehomme in the Seventh Arrondissement. Marie Quatrehomme was the first woman to win the coveted Meilleur Ouvrier de France title for cheese. Energetic and bright-eyed, she personally made our visit educational. She introduced us to cheeses that were floral, earthy, nutty or grassy. The shop is a swirling cornucopia of different smells and tastes, mushroomy, buttery and creamy, and some even barnyardy or meaty. Previously, we had no concept of the incredible range of flavors and aromas of cheese. Quatrehomme herself described their origins in France and the best seasons for each. We couldn't keep all of this together in our heads, so we let her select for us from the tastes we told her we liked the best. She wrapped the collection of small pieces in wax paper and rang us up. Amazing. An entire universe of cheese.

Not far away was Nicole Barthélémy's fascinating shop, possibly the most famous cheese shop in Paris. Barthélémy's is the official fromagerie for the Elysée Palace and the president's official dinners. Catherine Deneuve is a regular customer. We were a bit cautious because her reputation is that she does not suffer cheese neophytes gladly. We relied on our education from our last stop, Marie Quatrehomme, and strode in with false bravado. Barthélémy is a rather severe-looking woman who immediately convinced us that we should be terrified of her. She actually couldn't have been more charming. She helped advance our new Master's of Cheese degree and selected a cheese with a wonderful herbal fragrance of thyme and rosemary. Another full-flavored one with a strong taste of sweet hazelnuts and one with a spring-like taste of asparagus. Good enough for the president of France. Good enough for us.

Androuet was our next adventure. They have been in Paris since 1909. There are seven stores throughout the city. We tasted many cheeses from across the French landscape again. The salesperson found us an extraordinary cow's milk cheese with a hint of black truffles.

Our last stop was Laurent Dubois, another winner of the coveted Meilleur Ouvrier de France. They selected for us a goat's milk cheese with chives and one that smelled like perfumed flowers.

These four shops were extraordinary. A bit intimidating, but bewitching. No wonder the French believe that all one needs in life is a baguette, or two, some wonderful cheeses and a bottle of great French red wine. They are right. I fell in love with French cheeses on my first visit to Paris over 30 years ago. I spent years trying to find those enchanting tastes in high-end U.S. specialty cheese shops, to no avail.

Finding a great wine store was next. The French chain Nicolas, established in 1822, has over 400 stores across France and seems to be on every block in Paris. There are a number of sophisticated very high-end and expensive wine shops as well. Many Frenchmen and women actually buy their wine in their local supermarkets, where little-known but good-quality wines can be found for very reasonable prices. Many consider wine a staple of their diets and consume it at every meal.

For us, the most interesting wine store in all of Paris, and another place with good prices, was on the Left Bank in St.-Germain-des-Prés.

It is La Dernière Goutte (The Last Drop), run by Juan Sanchez. Juan himself is a Cuban-American, has a rare palate and is an extraordinary teacher. He is multilingual and holds two-hour wine classes in English in the stone-walled back room of his rustic boutique. The classes take you on a tour, using a big colorful map of France on the back wall, around all of the wine regions, and provide you with an opportunity to taste grapes and wines across the entire spectrum. He has free tastings on Fridays and Saturdays with the vin de propriétaire (estate bottled wine) winemakers themselves. Juan is very funny, incredibly knowledgeable, wonderfully disheveled, and never takes himself too seriously. He is always personally exploring all the regions of France to find great wines at reasonable prices. His staff is also very smart, and will help you choose a wine based on your tastes or assist with food and wine pairings. One assistant, Patty, is an aging hippie who won't remember you from one time to the next. This wine store is a must stop if you love wine. Worth the education about French wine even if you don't buy.

In Paris, we would sometimes substitute some good bread and cheese for one of our big restaurant lunches. Or sometimes a sandwich from one of Eric Kayser's boulangeries. Bread, cheese and wine are all you need to make Paris come alive. One could argue that you need to add foie gras, or oysters, or visits to chocolatiers and patisseries. Maybe. But bread, cheese and wine are the basic food groups in France that no one can do without. And when you take them on a picnic in a glorious Paris park, it becomes truly magical.

Explore the Luxembourg Gardens with its 60 acres of lush rolling lawns, French and English gardens, apple orchards, chestnut groves, geometric forest, sparkling ponds, the monumental Medici Fountain, and the song of children's laughter at the carousel, pony rides and puppet shows.

Wander the three-square-mile expanse of the Bois de Boulogne, taking in its multiple lakes and streams, picturesque waterfall, water lily pond, rose gardens, steeplechase hippodrome, and Asian gardens

CLOTHES IN EUROPE

We made a series of onerous and comical errors when we were packing for Europe. We thought we needed to pack different clothes for all four seasons. Big mistake. We also thought we needed to ensure that we had both casual and dressy clothes. Another big mistake. The result was two very large suitcases each, a small wheelie suitcase each and a briefcase each. Eight pieces in all. Totally unmanageable. A nightmare at airports

For me, this cornucopia of clothes included a business suit, three sports jackets, three pairs of khaki slacks, two pairs of gray dress slacks, two pairs of dress shoes, and five collared shirts. Nutty but true. For Lisa, it was three dresses, two blazers, three pairs of shoes, three sweaters, and several pairs of slacks. And this is just the stuff we eventually sent home. I know, what were we thinking? Keystone Cops-worthy material.

What we should have done is the following: One nice sports jacket or blazer. Three pairs of black jeans each or, worst case, dark blue jeans. You can get away with them even in the finest restaurants if you have a sports jacket. Two pairs of sneakers. One for rainy and snowy days, for walking to the gym and touring. You don't care what happens to them. The other pair should be black. These are your "formal shoes" that go with your black jeans for restaurants and such. One collared shirt for the fancy restaurants. Two polo/golf shirts. Two pairs of khaki shorts. I settled on four upscale black T-shirts. With the black jeans, black sneakers and sports jacket, it became my uniform. You also want four sets of shorts, tops, sports bras, socks, and a pair of sweatpants for cold weather en route to the gym. But that was all we needed, in addition to a winter ski coat and gloves for four months, a waterproof pullover with a hood for rainy days, and a bathing suit for Barcelona.

Lisa kept a few other items. She kept two sleeveless shirts and two with sleeves, one black and one white each, to match with a broad collection of inexpensive colorful scarves she bought from the countless street vendors in Rome and Florence. She also kept one fleece top to use for layering in the winter.

Lisa also bought a stylish purple Italian cotton Fedora and a black French beret so she would look like a local in Rome and Paris, but she sometimes came to regret it when so many tourists asked her for directions

So what do you send home? Basically everything that needs to be dry cleaned. In Europe, dry cleaning costs a fortune. Everything you bring must be washable.

Send home all of your shoes. Most of your collared shirts. Nice slacks. The majority of your dresses, blazers, sweaters and sports jackets.

We smartened up over time and sent clothes back home through Mail Boxes Etc. We sent some of our luggage back with our children upon their return to the U.S.

Roma, The Pantheon at Night

Roma, The Fountain of the Pantheon

Roma, Teatro di Marcello and Tempo di Apollo

Roma, The Colosseum

Roma, Ryan at the Colosseum

Roma, Lisa at Vini & Cucina

Roma, Alessandro and Sylvia with Lisa at Vini & Cucina

Roma, Street Musicians at Piazza Navona

Our Regular Lunch Table at the Campo de' Fiori Marketplace

Roma, The Communist Bar, Lara, the Bartender

Roma, The Communist Bar, Giancarlo, Lara, Lisa, Giulia and Marco

Roma, The Communist Bar, Joe, Paolo, Lisa and Diego

Roma, The Palimpsest, Monument of Victor
Emmanuel II from the Fori Imperiali

Roma, Nicole, the Bartender, Lisa, and
Gianmaria, the Chef, in our Gym

Roma, Monumento a Vittorio Emanuele II (The Wedding Cake)

Roma, Crowds at the Spanish Steps

Roma, Crowds at the Trevi Fountain

Roma, War Scenes from Trajan's Column

Roma, St. Peter's Square

Roma, Museo Atelier Canova Tadolini (Café)

Roma, Lisa and Joe Pose in the "Roman Holiday" Scooter Sign

Roma, Lisa Poses for the "Roman Holiday"
Hand in the Mouth of Truth Joke

Roma, A Communist Party Parade

Firenze, The Cathedral from our Airbnb Window

Firenze, The Cathedral in the Evening

Siena, Piazza del Campo and the Torre del Mangia Tower

Siena, The Duomo

Venezia, Piazza San Marco in the Fog

Venezia, The Grand Canal and a Gondola in the Winter Fog

Venezia, Our Gondola Heads Back to the Grand Canal

Venezia, Basilica di San Marco in the Winter Fog

Venezia, Lisa in the Back Canals in a Gondola

Paris, Cafés at Night

Paris, Notre-Dame, the Gothic Masterpiece

Paris, Arc de Triomphe

Paris, The Louvre

Paris, L'église de la Madeleine

Paris, Caitlin with an Artist in the Rain at Montmartre

Paris, the Iconic La Tour Eiffel

Paris, La Dernière Goute, Our Favorite Wine Store

Paris, Musée de L'Orangerie

Paris, Hemingway's Bar: La Rotonde

Paris, Le Père Lachaise Cemetery

Paris, Palais Garnier Opera House Interior

Paris, Le Petit Châtelet (Lisa's Favorite Restaurant)

Amsterdam, The Prinsengracht Canal

Nice, Marina Baie des Anges ("The Pyramids") Condos

Nice, The Village of Antibes

Orange, Théâtre Antique d'Orange

Châteauneuf-du-Pape, Le Château des Fines Roches

Châteauneuf-du-Pape, Sophie, Our Wine Tour Guide, with Lisa

Châteauneuf-du-Pape, Introduction to the Roger Sabon Winery

Barcelona, One Ocean Bar with Joe, José Maria, Lisa and José

Barcelona, The Bartenders in El Xampanyet with Lisa

Barcelona, El Xampanyet Bar

Barcelona, Fascinating La Sagrada Familia Statues

Barcelona, Quimet & Quimet Tapas Bar

Barcelona, Our Third Floor Airbnb (The Big Doors)

Barcelona, La Sagrada Familia

Barcelona, La Pedrera Rooftop

Barcelona, Basam's Girlfriend, Basam, and Lisa

Sevilla, Lisa in Her Flamenco Dress in our Airbnb Courtyard

Sevilla, Lisa in the Dress at the Bullfight

Sevilla, Tents in the Fairgrounds

Sevilla, A Table of Women in their Flamenco Dresses

Sevilla, Mosque-Cathedral of Cordoba

Our Gym in Barcelona Looking Out at the Mediterranean

RESTAURANTS IN PARIS

Lisa and I had been reasonably frugal at restaurants in Rome. It was natural and practical when the majority of them were simple trattorias but the meals were still excellent. Our plans were to be equally frugal in Barcelona and focus primarily on tapas-hopping across its many simple and equally excellent cafés. In Paris, however, we planned to be somewhat extravagant. Paris has the most three-star Michelin restaurants in Europe, by a lot. Michelin defines a three-star restaurant as "exceptional cuisine that is worth a special journey." Glorious. An orgasm of epicurean delight. An experience to die for. We were going to take advantage of these best-of-the-best restaurants while we were there. There were 10 total in Paris. We would select eight.

We continued our practice of having our big meal at lunch. When we went to these extraordinary restaurants in Paris, this had a special payoff. Most of these restaurants serve 10- to 12-course meals at both lunch and dinner, so we'd be losing nothing. The payoff was that the cost was often at least 50 percent less. A dinner at Guy Savoy could cost 350 euros per person. We were dying to go to these incredible restaurants, but not at that price. Lunch would be €110 per person. Even at that price, we would have to be frugal the rest of the week to stay within our budget.

The restaurants we selected were a who's who of world-class dining. Guy Savoy, Pierre Gagnaire, Alain Ducasse au Plaza Athénée, Pavillon Ledoyen, Epicure, Arpège, Astrance and L'Ambroisie. Each of their chefs is famous. This would be an adventure within an adventure. At first, Lisa thought we were crazy to do this, but she was not hard to convince. A once-in-a-lifetime experience.

We started with Guy Savoy. In a fascinating older building across the street from the Seine, we climbed a long, red-carpeted staircase to the second floor. The headwaiter seated us, introduced himself as Herbert, and remarked that it must be our first visit, because he remembers every guest he has served over the last 25 years. A slim, handsome man dressed impeccably, with perfectly coiffed salt-and-pepper hair, he explained that he had reserved us a special table at the floor-to-ceiling window because we were new clients. Impressive. Lisa and I looked out at the Seine. We could see the Pont Neuf, at the westernmost point of Ile de la Cité, and the Pont des Arts footbridge that leads to the Louvre, and then the Louvre itself. We looked directly at its most architecturally interesting building, the elegant facade of the Cour Carrée. It was the original medieval Louvre. Elsewhere in the room, there was an open fireplace and wonderful ornate molding on the walls. Lisa and I were at the best table at the best restaurant in Paris.

Lisa asked Herbert to help us select from the cornucopia of extraordinary choices for this 11-course extravaganza. He told her to choose her favorite items from the entire menu and he would create a special fixed price, custom menu, specifically for us. Amazing. It was no surprise the restaurant had the highest ratings for service of all of the best restaurants in Paris. Also, no wonder Herbert had been here for 25 years.

The appetizers arrived. Lisa's artichoke soup with black truffles and a layered, ruffled mushroom brioche was unbelievable. She moaned softly with every sip (and wasn't aware she was doing it). My fresh salmon cooked on a bed of dry ice with a sauce of lemon pearls was fantastic as well. But I needed to try the soup worth moaning over. Wow, it took over all of my senses at once. These two dishes were followed by oven-baked John Dory and a fillet of veal with its sweetbread. Next was a juicy venison served with hearty champignons and seared foie gras. Course after heavenly course for close to three hours. Then a delightful selection of Marie Quatrehomme cheeses from all over France. We finished with a chocolate and honey dessert. Then Herbert wheeled over the dessert cart. Too much. We were finished. No more. He was disappointed.

Finally, Herbert brought the chef out to meet us. Guy Savoy is a member of the Légion d'Honneur, the highest French order of merit, established by Napoleon in 1802. Other members have included Victor Hugo, Giuseppe Verdi, Marc Chagall and Auguste Rodin. Only the French would give its highest honor to a chef. Well not just any chef. He asked us if the meal was satisfactory. We told him it met our requirements. Actually, we told him it was our best meal ever. He was pleased. As we were leaving, Herbert asked us to join him again. We promised we would.

Our next adventure was with Alain Ducasse at the Plaza Athénée, a historic luxury hotel near the Champs-Elysées. Ducasse is only one of two chefs to hold 21 Michelin stars. Another extraordinary meal, highlighted by scallops and black truffles with cauliflower and Comté in a pastry shell. Lisa had Atlantic sea bass with clementine confit and white asparagus. We ordered different courses in every restaurant but shared everything. Service was always excellent.

In his famous restaurant, Pierre Gagnaire prepares dishes widely described as "jarring juxtapositions of flavors, tastes, textures and ingredients." He has been called off-the-wall in his combinations. We had a thinly sliced abalone with poached duck, foie gras and figatellu sausage. It seemed as if the bizarre collection of tastes couldn't possibly work together, but it was wonderful. That is how Gagnaire does everything. His restaurant has been rated third-best in the world three times.

The Pavillon Ledoyen is a glorious two-story pavilion situated in a garden off the eastern end of the Champs-Elysées. It is one of the oldest restaurants in Paris. Napoleon and Josephine dined here, as did Degas, Monet and Zola. We sat at a window again and gazed out into the gardens. Yannick Alléno, the charismatic chef, served up a wonderful sea urchin soup in a charred grapefruit, scallop ravioli with caviar, and a steamed turbot with green pea risotto with beluga lentils. Another breathtaking experience.

Epicure is located in the majestic Le Bristol hotel in the heart of the fashion district. Our table looked out on the well-tended private Bristol garden. Magnificent dishes again: macaroni stuffed with black truffles, artichoke and duck foie gras, with an aged parmesan gratin. Spicy duck breast with a carpaccio of fresh figs. You would think we would get tired of eating fabulous food all the time. Or even once a week. But the days we had these spectacular lunches needed to be spaced out. And we needed to walk home and sleep it off. It was actually overwhelming.

Alain Passard has created the extraordinary, vegetable-friendly restaurant Arpège. It is directly across from the Musée Rodin. The vegetables are grown in the chef's biodynamic kitchen gardens. Passard delivers extremely creative vegetable dishes like tomato gazpacho paired with a celery and mustard ice cream, beet tartare, and cévennes onion gratin with black truffles. Every one of the 10 courses was a wonderful surprise. We finished up with a superb lamb and duck dish and a visit by the chef. Arpège is rated 19th best in the world.

Pascal Barbot's 12-course lunch at Astrance for 70 euros is the best high-end value in Paris. The mushroom and foie gras tart marinated in verjus is really something. Try the oh-so-pink slice of tuna surrounded by a vivid collection of vegetables, almond milk sauce and bergamot coulis. This is No. 18 in the world.

We then returned to Guy Savoy. We had to tell Herbert he was the best in Paris, if not the world. He was pleased. Lisa leaned over and whispered to me that this was a bit of a transmutation from the food we ate for dinner growing up. Because our mothers both worked, we became accustomed to a potpourri of Dinty Moore Beef Stew from a can, Chun King Chow Mein from a can, Mrs. Paul's frozen fish sticks, Morton frozen pot pies. Lisa said it was a big deal when she got to pick out her own frozen TV dinner. We started laughing hysterically and Herbert rushed over to see if something was wrong. No, we explained. We were just telling old funny stories. He made sure this experience was as wonderful as the first. A special host in a special place.

So, were all these restaurants worth it? Absolutely. The greatest collection of meals in our entire lives, all enjoyed over the course of eight weeks. Were we spoiled? Absolutely. Extraordinary tastes, extraordinary combinations, extraordinary wine pairings, extraordinary service. It actually was an overwhelming experience. We needed a full week to recover from each of these culinary adventures. But every time we are in Paris, we will make a return trip or two.

The Surprise
Telephone Call

We walked slowly along the Seine. We passed our favorite bookstore in Paris, the famous Shakespeare and Company, and entered Lisa's favorite little French restaurant, Le Petit Châtelet at 39 Rue de la Bûcherie. This was our third visit. Because we were in the cold of January, and we normally arrived at noon, it was always fairly empty. It is a small two-story wood-paneled building with a cute tan and white striped awning, almost hidden by the tall buildings that surround it. It looks like a Paris bistro right out of the 1800s.

Inside it has a warm provincial decor and a series of paintings of its exterior, made by assorted artists over the years. It has an authentic ambience. Beautiful music is always playing. We sat at our usual window seats, and we stared across the Seine at Notre-Dame.

We ordered from the chalkboard menu that they placed on an empty chair at our table. The handsome, curly-haired waiter was very friendly and welcomed us back. He brought a plate of fresh grilled bread, butter, a carafe of house wine and a bottle of sparkling water to our table. Our first course was Lisa's favorite dish in Paris, a large ceramic bowl of escargots in a mushroom cream sauce topped with puff pastry. I lost her when she dived into it. She was unaware of the soft moans she made as she consumed it. It was the perfect dish for the cold of Paris's winter. There are other nice dishes that they prepare on their wood-fired grill in the back — lamb skewers, rib-eye steaks and more — but this is the dish that continued to bring us back there.

Then my phone rang. I rarely received phone calls in Europe. It was my brother Tom. He was in a panic. I couldn't hear him clearly with the music and I went outside to talk, but I left without my coat and I was freezing.

He explained that he was in Florida, at the hospital with my mother. What? But she was healthy and in good spirits when I last saw her. We had talked often via video from Europe on FaceTime, on the iPad my brother Charlie had bought her. Tom explained that she was in the hospital, and that doctors had found Stage 4 esophageal cancer. Stage 4 is almost always fatal.

Mom had been unable to eat or drink for two days, and had called my cousin Victor, who lives in the same retirement complex. He took her to the hospital. Oh my God! But Tom said there was more. She had received a feeding tube in a procedure called a percutaneous endoscopic gastrostomy because she was so weak and had lost so much weight. But there had been complications and she was in intensive care with pneumonia. She may die.

Oh my God. My mother was in intensive care in Florida, and here I was in Paris. Lisa and I rushed back to our Airbnb. She started making calls to try to get us on a flight to Fort Lauderdale. She finally found one we could afford. The next morning, we packed our bags and rushed to the airport. We were scared.

Upon arrival, we took a taxi to my mom's home and met Tom, who had just returned from the hospital in my mom's car. He was nervous and disheveled. We all headed back over to the hospital and sped up to intensive care. Mom was conscious again but moaning, as if she was in pain. She had lost 20 pounds and was appallingly thin. Her skin was gray. Our hearts sank. She was having difficulty breathing. But we had gotten there in time.

She was also upset. She told us that when Tom had gone to pick us up, a doctor came by, asked if she had a living will, and advised her to get her affairs in order. She asked if she could have surgery to remove the tumor. No, the doctor said, the cancer was too advanced, and she would not survive the operation.

Tom had to return home to New Jersey the next day. He had been the Dunkin Donuts king, bringing doughnuts and coffee to the intensive care nurses to stay in their good graces. He had held down the fort when Mom was at the greatest risk, but he had to get back to work.

My mom began to recover somewhat, and the nurses wanted us to walk her around the halls with her oxygen tank and IV pole to get her circulatory and respiratory systems moving again and help drain her lungs. Once she started complaining about the hospital staff, we knew she was feeling better.

My mom, Barbara, was the 87-year-old, 5-foot-1-inch, 100-pound, overly tanned, hyperactive, driven, passionate, funny, successful, independent, creative and occasionally combative youngest child of poor Ukrainian and Russian immigrants. After my dad died, she flew by herself between their homes in Florida and New Jersey every year. She still painted all the time, golfed occasionally, went on cruises with friends, hosted the local ladies' card games, and was the chauffeur for all of the women in the neighborhood older than she was. That last part was scary.

I agreed with her that the care she was receiving was lacking in many ways. Hospital systems that surround retirement villages in our country are often poor. The situation was similar when my dad, Joe, fell ill with lung cancer years before. My folks were in their other retirement home, in Toms River, N.J. We tried to move him to live with us for his treatment, but he wouldn't hear of it. He wanted to be close to his own home and to be independent. We honored his wishes. But we believed that lapses in the care he received hastened his death.

Stronger though she was, Barbara really wasn't recovering. She had an inoperable tumor that filled her esophagus and would soon be putting additional pressure on her windpipe and breathing. She refused chemotherapy and radiation because of the pain and side effects she had seen my dad go through. We told her we would try one last option. We would reach out to a world-class esophageal surgeon at the prestigious Hospital of the University of Pennsylvania. We would send her records there and see if there was any chance that my mom's tumor could be removed by this doctor's team. She got very excited and kept telling her nurses that her son was getting the greatest doctor in the country and that this doctor would save her.

Presently, the hospital asked us to move Barbara for rehabilitation at a different facility down the road. I had never noticed before, but her entire town was filled with rehabilitation facilities. They surrounded the hospital like locusts.

We moved my mom into her new room, but it was a disturbing environment. Patients kept yelling for help, and most seemed to be ignored. Lisa and I spent 12 hours a day there and it wasn't enough. I had an emotional outburst one evening and my mom gave me a "timeout." Seriously, she told me I was misbehaving and I had to go sit in her car. A 64-year-old man in a timeout? I did it.

Still, Barbara had a wonderful personal support system. My cousin Victor, who was nearly her age, and his wife, Libby, came every day to visit. They look like gracefully aging movie stars. My brothers, Charlie and Tom, and their wives, Isabel and Holly, called every day. All the grandchildren — Jen, Caroline, Alissa, Caitlin, Ryan, Brendan and Kyle — called her frequently. Her retirement village neighbors called her often as well. Millie, her best friend from New Jersey, called every day with news from the neighborhood. Barbara was excited and animated on the telephone most of the day. Another close friend, Eileen, rode her bicycle two miles to visit every day. She told us not to worry about her; she rode only on the sidewalk. One day she brought a priest to give my mom last rites. I thought it might unnerve her, but it gave her peace.

With all the attention, Mom's spirits improved. She was looking healthier. Her face regained its color. She told everyone who would listen that Lisa and I were going to take her to have her tumor removed at the University of Pennsylvania and that she would be fine. She would then recover with Tom and Holly, who were saving their guest bedroom for her.

My mom was afraid to be alone at night, however. She still had trouble breathing. She complained that no one responded when she buzzed the night staff. She just didn't trust them. We hired a private nurse for the night shift. But the rehabilitation staff was great. They had her riding a stationary bike. She lifted tiny weights. She did leg exercises in bed. She was looking and feeling better. We would take her outside in her wheelchair to get some sun and fresh air.

A few days later, word came back from the Hospital of the University of Pennsylvania. It wasn't good. Her tumor was inoperable. We were devastated. When we told her, she said she expected the worst because it had taken them so long to respond. She showed no emotion. She was stoic. She looked out the window.

Still bent on recovering, Barbara decided she wanted to leave Florida and go to my brother Tom's place in New Jersey. Lisa and I would accompany her. But the doctors would not let her fly. They said her lung capacity was diminished from the pneumonia and she needed so much oxygen, she could not be on a plane. We fought over it. She was insistent.

Holly found the answer: a stretch Mercedes ambulance that traveled with a dedicated nurse and two EMTs as drivers. Perfect. Could we withstand a 22-hour ride? We had to.

Before we left, we had to tell Barbara that we were really taking her to a hospice. She had previously told us to never let her go to a hospice. She was crestfallen, and we were brokenhearted. We showed her pictures on our computer of how beautiful it was. It was on the top of a hill on a horse farm in the country, and her room looked down on the horses and lakes below. The horses would come right up to her sliding back door. Barbara was very sad. But she said she understood that Tom and Holly could not take care of her with all of her medical challenges. She knew she needed constant attention.

We stopped back at her home and packed up. We brought her favorite DVD set, the first season of "Murder She Wrote" with

Angela Lansbury. We stopped at a liquor store and bought four bottles of chardonnay, a corkscrew and some plastic cups for the ride. The ambulance staff lifted her into the luxurious car. She told the nurse she wouldn't ride facing backwards, that the headlights from behind would annoy her. But the nurse said it was safer, and Mom agreed.

Barbara never slept for the 22 hours. Lisa and I slept only five minutes at a time, between telling old stories with her and changing the DVDs for "Murder She Wrote." We saw every episode, some more than once. We unfortunately memorized who committed every crime.

Mom whispered to me between episodes that life wasn't fair. She remembered that the day before my dad died, he and I were drinking vodka and tonics all day, telling funny old stories about our family, and he was laughing so hard he would cough. That's how she wanted to die, she said, angry that she couldn't even drink liquids anymore.

When we finally arrived at the hospice near my brother Tom's house in northern New Jersey, it looked like a ranch out West. It was spacious and beautiful. Her private room was as big as the living room and dining room combined in her little retirement home. Tom, Holly and their son, Kyle, greeted us. The nurses all came out to greet us as well. The facilities, the spacious kitchen, the glorious living room with an enormous fireplace, and her large, modern, colorful bedroom were even better than the pictures. She essentially had a private nurse, but all the nurses were thoughtful, upbeat and welcoming. Holly and Tom had covered the walls with photographs of our entire family and my mom's life over the years.

We spent three days there getting Mom acclimated. She started to relax. She had talks with the nurses, visited other patients, watched MSNBC all day and yelled at Donald Trump on the television. My brother Charlie and his wife came to visit her. Our children, Caitlin, Ryan and Brendan, also came. Tom, Holly and Kyle were there taking shifts every day.

When we asked the nurses how long she had to live, they told us it was impossible to tell. It could be two weeks, it could be six months. We had now been with her for 12 days. She was comfortable, happy and animated, and surrounded by loved ones. Visitors all the time. We decided there was not much more we could do. With very heavy hearts, we returned to Paris.

We were back only a week when Tom and Holly invited all of our cousins for a big party with Mom on the weekend. Whole families came from different parts of New Jersey. She dialed us from her iPad using the FaceTime app. She turned the iPad around to show us everyone who was there. Mary, Carol, Joanie, Don — on and on. The room was packed, very loud, and filled with laughter. Everyone told funny stories about Mom's life. She kept interrupting people by telling stories she thought were funnier. She laughed so loud she sounded like a donkey braying. She held up the iPad so it was facing the group and made me tell the "timeout" story of her son of 64 years being sent to the car, and everyone thought it was hilarious. The party went on for hours.

Finally, a nurse stopped in and said my mom was getting tired and everyone had to leave. Before they left, she thanked her guests and told them it was the best day of her life. Thank you. Thank you, she repeated to everyone as they slowly left her room. She thanked Lisa and me and turned off the iPad. She died in her sleep that night. She was a wonderful woman and had a wonderful, fulfilling life. She also got her wish about her last day. But without the vodka and tonics.

The Return to Paris

Lisa and I returned from New Jersey and my mom, but we really struggled to reacclimate ourselves to Paris, Europe and just being away from home. The Paris winter was still overcast, cold and dreary. Our apartment felt especially dreary, with insufficient daylight inside in a winter of insufficient daylight outdoors. We remained in such a funk about my mom. We couldn't escape it.

One evening I told Lisa to get dressed up and we would have a great time at our favorite jazz bar with one of our favorite bartenders: Max, the tall, handsome German. She agreed. She put on a stylish blue and purple skirt and jacket outfit with a matching scarf and hat, and jewelry she had bought in Rome at a very fashionable store. She was all decked out and ready again for Paris.

We began the six short blocks to Café Laurent and set out down the dark cobblestone street behind the Church of St.-Germain-des-Prés. Lifting her foot to step onto the sidewalk, Lisa tripped, fell and knocked herself out. I quickly pulled her up in a panic and leaned her against a tall wrought-iron fence. Her eyes opened briefly, looked at me blankly, and then closed again, and she crumpled back to the ground in a semi-fetal position. My body chilled and I yelled for help.

Two passing Parisians asked if I wanted an ambulance. Yes, I implored. They called for us. I dragged Lisa up again from the ground and leaned her against the fence again, holding her there. I pleaded with her to open her eyes. Talk to me, talk to me. Nothing. I was terrified. What could it be? A stroke. A heart attack. She never had any warning symptoms of either. Lisa crumpled again even as I tried to hold her against the fence with all of my strength. She was dead weight. I got down on the ground and kept talking to her.

The ambulance arrived, and the EMTs and I helped her in. She was awake again, but she kept repeating, "What am I doing here? What am I doing here? How did I get here?" The ambulance staff told her that her vitals were good but that her blood pressure was very high. They wanted to take her to the hospital, but she refused. "Please don't take me to the hospital, Joe. Don't let them take me to the hospital," she implored. "I am fine." I suggested she take their advice and go there. She repeated that she wasn't going under any circumstances, that I should take her to the jazz club as we had planned. She was unmovable. The EMTs said it was O.K. I helped her out of the ambulance and we walked the short distance to the club.

There, she had a sparkling water and we tried to figure out what had happened. I told her I had thought she was dying. It was the most terrifying moment of my life. She said she'd been thinking about how incredibly stressful my mom's sickness and death had been, coming as it did so soon after the death of her father just five weeks before we left for Europe. She hadn't known how much the confluence of the two events had affected her. It made her think about the ephemeral nature of life. And then she thought about how we were completely alone in Europe by ourselves. Her mind was just whirling over and over about all of it, and then she tripped, fell, hit her head and blacked out. It had completely overwhelmed her.

Lisa was fine after that discussion. Such a thing had never happened to her before, and never happened again. For me, it was the scariest moment of my life, down on the ground, alongside her unconscious body on a dark, cold night in Paris.

Paris Churches

Notre-Dame de Paris, meaning Our Lady of Paris, for us is the icon of the city. Notre-Dame's home is Ile de la Cité, the cradle of Paris. It is geographically at the heart of the capital, a supreme masterpiece of French Gothic architecture. This medieval Catholic cathedral is one of the largest and best-known Catholic churches in France and the world. It has been a source of visual and literary inspiration over the centuries. By design, or by chance, we walked past it every day, sometimes more than once. We seemed to be unconsciously drawn to it.

Notre-Dame's groundbreaking was in 1163 and it took over 180 years to complete. It was one of the first churches to be supported by flying buttresses. It is 420 feet long and 157 feet wide, and the twin towers soar 226 feet into the heavens with its single spire reaching 300 feet. The majestic towers are visible from all over Paris. We occasionally used them as a compass to guide our explorations.

Emmanuel, the great bell in the south tower, weighs 13 tons and its clapper alone weighs a thousand pounds. Emmanuel rings on the hour, and 5 seconds later is accompanied by the church's nine other bells. These rhythmic, harmonious sounds were a continuous inspiration for us, wandering this great city.

Statues surround the exterior and act as column supports and waterspouts, famous gargoyles designed for water runoff. But the centerpiece of this grand church is the central Catherine window, or rose window, that is nearly 33 feet across. Representative of Gothic architecture, it is a wheel window divided by spokes radiating from the center. The north rose of Notre-Dame has, at its center, the

Blessed Virgin Mary and the Christ Child surrounded by prophets and saints. It has one of the highest ratios of glass and stone of any rose window. Magnificent colored streams of light fill the church on sunny days.

The organ boasts 8,000 pipes, the most of any organ in France. The concerts on Sunday afternoons are a must. The deep, rich sounds encircled and engulfed Lisa and me.

After that description, you must be convinced that Notre-Dame is our favorite church in Paris. We love it but it's not. That distinction belongs to the Gothic architectural marvel that graces the opposite end of Ile de la Cité: Sainte-Chapelle, or the Holy Chapel. It is a royal chapel in the Gothic style within the medieval Palais de la Cité, the residence of the kings of France until the 14th century.

The exterior is gray and austere. It is devoid of the flying buttresses and major sculptures of Notre-Dame. After entering the church and climbing the spiral stairs to the upper level, you emerge into a sweeping, bejeweled 50-foot-tall stained-glass house, glowing red, blue, green and violet. It is a breathtaking Gothic wonderland. Time stood still here. The single greatest visual joy in Paris. Sainte-Chapelle has one of the most extensive 13th-century stained-glass collections anywhere in the world. These stained-glass windows are the oldest to survive in Paris.

The church has 16 50-foot stained-glass windows decorated with 1,134 religious scenes over a glazed area of 6,672 square feet. They circle the room. This amazing iconographic program covers these windows from floor to ceiling with the New Testament stories featuring Christ's Passion, the Infancy of Christ, the Life of John the Evangelist and others. The Old Testament scenes include portions from Genesis, Exodus, Numbers/Leviticus, Joshua/Deuteronomy, and Judges. The stories embedded in these glorious windows mesmerized Lisa and me. We were enveloped in a sea of bright pastel colors. There is no other place in the world like this.

Another great visit was to the Basilique du Sacré-Coeur, or Sacred Heart. Its three majestic pearl-colored domes overlook and protect the city from atop the summit of Montmartre, the highest point of the city. Sun-drenched by day and brightly lit by night, it is a constant feature of the Paris skyline, gently gracing the horizon.

The interior contains one of the largest mosaics in the world, which depicts Jesus Christ with outstretched arms. Lisa and I climbed to the top of the dome for its spectacular panoramic view of the city. We could see all the locations we had visited, the Eiffel Tower, the Panthéon, everything.

There are other wonderful churches in Paris. St.-Eustache is a beautiful Renaissance church adorned by stained-glass windows and a number of important statues and artworks. St.-Étienne has lovely stained-glass as well and draws an overflow crowd for its spectacular organ concert after Sunday Mass. And St.-Sulpice is another wonderful church. It is worth a visit to see the Delacroix murals alone.

A PASSION FOR
PHILOSOPHERS AND WRITERS

The Panthéon wasn't on our list of priorities when we arrived in Paris. When we finally went to explore the Latin Quarter to see it, we were surprised and delighted. It was modeled after the Pantheon in Rome and is of the Neo-Classical style. It has a magnificent dome on a massive portico with richly detailed Corinthian columns. It was designed initially as a church and was transformed into a secular mausoleum that holds the remains of distinguished French citizens. Who it held was our big surprise.

Washington has monuments to George Washington, Thomas Jefferson, Abraham Lincoln and Franklin Delano Roosevelt. They were among our greatest political leaders. Paris has Les Invalides, which is Napoleon's tomb.

The heroes of the Panthéon tell us a different story about the French culture. In the crypt below are the tombs of their greatest philosophers, people like Jean-Jacques Rousseau, who was a leader in modern political and educational thought. He wrote "The Social Contract" and "Discourse on the Origin of Inequality." His political philosophy strongly influenced the Age of Enlightenment in France and had an important impact on the American and French Revolutions. "The Social Contract" was based on the premise that loyalty to the good of all men must be a supreme commitment by everyone. His treatise "Emile, or On Education" was based on his belief that education needs to be carried out in a holistic way with the goal of creating engaged, active citizens.

Philosophers like François–Marie Arouet, known by his nom de plume, Voltaire, are also buried there. Voltaire wrote "Candide" and was known for his advocacy of freedom of religion, freedom of speech, and the separation of church and state. The philosophers of the Age of Enlightenment had a big impact on the thinking of Benjamin Franklin, Thomas Jefferson and James Madison in the United States.

The Panthéon is the final resting place of many of France's greatest and best-known writers as well. Victor Hugo, who wrote "Les Misérables" and "The Hunchback of Notre-Dame," is interred there. Alexandre Dumas, who wrote "The Three Musketeers" and "The Count of Monte Cristo," is also buried there. Émile Zola, who was twice nominated for the Nobel Prize in Literature, is there as well.

There is no significant memorial in the United States where we honor our great philosophers and writers, the ones who influenced our nation's values and thinking. We have great philosophers like William James, Ralph Waldo Emerson and Henry David Thoreau, but no Panthéon to honor them.

This respect for intellectuals and writers that almost reaches reverence doesn't stop at the Panthéon. Paris Descartes University honors René Descartes, the father of modern Western philosophy. The school is in the Latin Quarter, and he is buried nearby, down the boulevard in the Church of St.-Germain-des-Prés.

Montesquieu, another major philosopher, wrote "The Spirit of the Laws." His ideas about the separation of powers between the branches of government formed the basis of the U.S. Constitution. He is interred in the famous Church of St.-Sulpice, at the edge of the Latin Quarter not far from the Panthéon. And the philosopher Denis Diderot, who wrote the seminal "Encyclopedia," in which he hoped to include all of the world's knowledge, is buried in the Church of St.-Roch. The Paris Diderot multidisciplinary university is named for him.

A very significant portion of our constitution, rules of law, principles and beliefs came from these gentlemen, and most Americans have no idea who they were. But all Parisians do.

Even modern-day existentialist philosophers like Jean-Paul Sartre and Simone de Beauvoir, and great writers like Marcel Proust and Honoré de Balzac, have Parisians making pilgrimages to their graves in the Montparnasse and Père Lachaise Cemeteries. It is their respect for the intellectual tradition.

But it doesn't end there. Parisians remain passionate about knowledge, books and bookstores to this day. Most of our U.S. bookstores are being slowly closed down, but not in France. A French law passed in 1981 prevented bookstores from reducing their prices by more than 5 percent. It keeps them all in business. Another law limits Paris bookstores' rent increases. The small bookstore lives on, and Amazon is kept at bay in France. A New York Times article on bookstores in Paris quotes one bookstore owner, "There are two things you don't throw out in France, bread and books."

This passion for continuous learning extends to the entire Paris society. One campus puts out a large stack of used books on sunny days, and all the books have new homes by mid-morning.

Parisians love a passionate discussion about philosophy, great writers, government, everything. Vive la France. It is a clear differentiator for its culture. The experience forced us to reread these great philosophers. I don't remember a focus on them in high school, although they are the foundation of our society. It's amazing we had to go to Paris to discover how we became the country we are. One of the real unknown values of the trip. And you can get all the books you need to catch up on this at the greatest English bookstore in Paris, the famous Shakespeare and Company. I went to the store and bought Voltaire, Rousseau and Montesquieu, all for the first time.

The 'Merde' Capital
of Europe

Paris, La Ville Lumière, The City of Lights: 296 illuminated sites at night, 33 illuminated bridges. The sparkling Eiffel Tower off on the horizon. A string of lights 2.1 kilometers long from Place de la Concorde to the Arc de Triomphe, with 450 trees illuminated at Christmas.

Those are everyone's favorite memories of Paris. Or Paris in their imagination. But today's Paris makes one cautious about looking up to the sky for inspiration while breezily walking down their breathtaking boulevards. That's because there are some 300,000 dogs in Paris. They have more dogs per capita than any other big city in Western Europe. French bulldogs, Lowchens, Briards, Papillons, Barbets, Picardy Spaniels, Pyrenean Mountain dogs, Braque du Bourbonnais, and the iconic poodles. Too many to count. Small, big, short and fat. Mostly small, though. You weave your way around them everywhere you go. Dog walkers with seven dogs on overlapping, tangled leashes. Even the homeless have dogs curled up and sharing their dirty mattresses and blankets. Sometimes multiple dogs.

These dogs deposit 16 tons of waste per day on Paris city streets, according to various estimates, and a majority of owners choose not to pick it up. Dreadful. We were all too aware of this as we walked to our gym every morning through our residential St.-Germain neighborhood.

For a time, the Brigade de Propreté et Incivilités (Cleanliness and Anti-Social Behavior Brigade) had responsibility for the clean-up. The agency had a team of 70 green "motocrotte" or "caninette" motorcycle drivers outfitted with vacuum cleaners. They drove through the city every day to suck all of this up. In 2002, the city, due to a budget crisis, decided it was too expensive and closed the agency. The city then imposed a fine of up to 450 euros on the dog owners. But the Paris police is a unit of the national police, and the national police do not put a priority on policing dogs and their owners.

To put this all in perspective, while dog owners in Britain bought 1.85 million Beco Pets Poop Bags in 2015 and Italian dog owners bought 800,000, the French took home just 3,600, the company found. As a result, as many as 650 people a year either break bones or are hospitalized by slipping and falling because of Paris's dog waste left on the streets.

So when walking down Paris's streets, keep your eyes on the sidewalk immediately ahead of you. Avert your eyes from the beautiful Eiffel Tower sparkling in the distance. Don't let yourself be mesmerized by the beauty of Notre-Dame's Gothic architecture, stained-glass windows and flying buttresses calling to you from across the Seine. Avoid being entranced by Sacré-Coeur's magnificent domes glowing on the summit of Montmartre. Just put one foot ahead of the other, and keep looking down.

And you always had the misperception that Parisians hate Americans. That's not true. They actually hate authority, and possibly each other. That's why Paris is the "Merde Capital of Europe."

THE GHOST OF ERNEST
HEMINGWAY TOUR

We were always fascinated by the stories of Paris in the 1920s and 1930s and all of the great European and American expatriate writers. There were Ernest Hemingway, F. Scott Fitzgerald, Gertrude Stein, James Joyce, Ezra Pound, John Dos Passos, and later Henry Miller. They were the Lost Generation. Hemingway wrote about many of them in his memoir, "A Movable Feast." Hemingway in Paris became his own mythological set of tales, almost like the "Washington slept here" stories from the American Revolutionary War. We combed "A Movable Feast" and the guidebooks to put together the definitive collection of his most renowned locations. We looked for the authentic cafés and bars where Hemingway spent his mornings and afternoons writing, and evenings drinking with this unique set of quirky and brilliant characters. These cafés and brasseries were all over the city, as you might expect. The greatest concentration was clustered in two main neighborhoods: Montparnasse, in the 14th Arrondissement, and St.-Germain, in the Sixth Arrondissement.

One couldn't spend three months in Paris without re-creating the environment of the Lost Generation. Most of the cafés were said to be unchanged in the last hundred years. The ghosts of Hemingway and his confrères were begging us to take the journey. We would most likely meet these other great writers, and often their artist friends, along the way. Time to put on our drinking shoes.

We awoke to a cold, overcast, steel-gray Paris morning. Even in winter, there were more of these days than we expected. We dressed, grabbed our umbrellas, and headed out. We walked briskly past the beautiful Luxembourg Palace and through the Luxembourg Gardens, Hemingway's favorite park for reading, writing, strolling with his son Bumby's carriage, and secretly hunting pigeons in his poorer early days in Paris. We walked through the beautifully landscaped 60-acre grounds, passing countless gray statues, monuments and fountains in the nearly empty park. We exited the back of the park and then traveled through the neatly coiffed Jardin des Grands-Explorateurs directly behind it. We then found our first destination, La Closerie des Lilas, a café at 171 Boulevard du Montparnasse. Its name means small, enclosed lilac garden. It was one of the hearts of intellectual and artistic life in Paris.

It was elegant and charming. Built in 1847, it was frequented beginning in the 1860s by Monet, Renoir, Pissarro, Bazille and Sisley — a group of artists who revolted against the academic painting standards of the time and were later called the Impressionists. They were joined by their literary friend Émile Zola and his painter friend since childhood, Paul Cézanne.

Cubism was born here in 1905 with the painters Picasso, Braque and later Matisse. And in the 1920s, it became the home of the Lost Generation: Hemingway, Fitzgerald, Stein and Beckett. Another generation of artists who called this little oasis home.

Hemingway would begin his day with coffee at this café. It was here that he wrote the novel "The Sun Also Rises" and the stories "The Big Two-Hearted River" and "Soldier's Home." He would change his seat to stay in the sun as it moved around the building, or sit on the beautiful side terrace covered in trees, shrubs and vines. It was here that Fitzgerald first read him a draft of "The Great Gatsby."

We stopped for a wonderful lunch here of oysters, steak tartare, pommes frites and a bottle of Bordeaux. One could feel the ghosts of all of the incredible history here. Multiple generations. Decades of creative energy swirling around. Their voices, their laughter, their arguments. Hemingway wrote about it in "A Movable Feast," but it preceded him by 60 years. He inherited all of that wonderful energy.

After an espresso, we wandered to the piano bar on the other side of the café. We discovered one-by-three-inch brass nameplates at the corner of every table and in front of every bar seat with the engraved names of literary figures. Hemingway's was at the bar. Photos from those days surrounded us, including one of Hemingway in his World War I uniform. Other names surprised us: Jean-Paul Sartre and Simone de Beauvoir. Yet a fourth generation of intellectuals, the existentialists. What a fitting metaphor for all those who transformed their artistic fields here.

The restaurant is continuing this intellectual and creative tradition. Every year, they award the Closerie des Lilas Prize, a literary prize for women. The excellence continues.

While we were in the restaurant, it began raining. We gathered our umbrellas and turned right down Boulevard du Montparnasse, a four-lane thoroughfare. The rain picked up as we proceeded. We were walking toward four of the most famous night spots of the Lost Generation: Le Select, La Coupole, Le Dôme and La Rotonde. They are across from one another at the "four corners" of Montparnasse where Boulevard du Montparnasse and Boulevard Raspail cross. This is one of the most mythical neighborhoods in Paris. Montparnasse is named after Mount Parnassus, the home of the nine muses of arts and sciences in Greek mythology. Some believe it was named specifically for the legendary home of Apollo, the god of poetry. It is a short two blocks from Montparnasse Cemetery, where Sartre, de Beauvoir, Baudelaire, Beckett, Ionesco and many other artists and intellectuals are buried. We planned to stop and have a leisurely cocktail in each of these establishments on Boulevard du Montparnasse and re-create Hemingway's journey.

Le Select at No. 99 is woven throuhout "The Sun Also Rises." Jake Barnes and Lady Brett Ashley have a drink here, and Jake returns another three times. Photos from the 1920s show it hasn't changed at all since Hemingway's time. It was also frequented by Beckett,

Sartre, de Beauvoir and Picasso. Harold Stearns, the American expatriate editor, writes in "Confessions of a Harvard Man" that it was a "madhouse of drunks, semi-drunks and sober maniacs." It is a simple, earthy, serious drinker's bar. An Irish whiskey "neat" seemed appropriate. The bartender was gruff and gave gravelly one-word answers. We didn't stay long.

Across the street at No. 105 is La Rotonde. Sweeping red awnings, matching red wicker chairs and an enormous gold sign draw you in. It was a meeting place for Leon Trotsky and the Russian revolutionaries in the early 1910s. Hemingway wrote upon discovering it in 1922, "The scum of Greenwich Village, New York, has been skimmed off and deposited here in large ladles. ... They are nearly all loafers expending the energy that an artist puts into his creative work in talking about what they are going to do, and condemning the work of all artists that have gained any degree of recognition." It was also frequented by Gershwin, Picasso and Fitzgerald.

Le Dôme at No. 108 curves around its broad corner location. It has one of the longest and most colorful histories of all of these cafés. Opened in 1898, it was originally the home of Paris's bohemian artists and their models. Paul Gauguin, Amedeo Modigliani, Picasso and others made this their meeting place. After World War I it became the Anglo-American café that was so wildly popular with writers, journalists and the next generation of artists. Hemingway, Ezra Pound, Henry Miller, Sinclair Lewis, Beckett, Eric Rohmer and Eugene Ionesco numbered among its many locals. It is staffed by tuxedoed waiters and has a comfortably old-fashioned décor with colorful Tiffany lamps and potted plants. Its outside terrace reaches across the broad sidewalk in two directions, nearly to the street. In the old black-and-white photos, the small tables are packed with people engaging in lively discussions.

Finally, at No. 102 is the wonderful Art Deco La Coupole. It fills the center of the block. A massive brasserie and restaurant, it became a jumping dance hall with musicians at night. It was decorated in

1927 by 27 Art Deco painters from Montmartre, including Marc Chagall. Their beautiful frescoes top a fascinating series of square green marble pillars throughout the room, as well as the pilasters along the side and back walls. Large black-and-white photos of the exciting parties and limitless energy of those days are scattered about the room. It was a culturally and intellectually diverse and dramatic crowd that filled the dance hall. Hemingway, Henry Miller and Anaïs Nin were joined by the singer Edith Piaf, the singer and dancer Josephine Baker, and the artists Marc Chagall, Georges Braque, Yves Klein, Fernand Léger and Alberto Giacometti. And of course, Sartre and de Beauvoir were frequently there. James Joyce would sip Irish whiskey at the long mirrored bar. What a blast that must have been. We ordered two brut rosé Champagnes and bathed in the atmosphere: the creative juices, the energy, the sharing of ideas and criticism alike. This place was great. We really felt as if the spirits of these cultural revolutionaries still lived here.

Standing under the awning of Le Dôme, we scanned these four famous establishments one last time. A multicultural, multidimensional history of decades of artistic, literary and philosophical greatness is layered here. Now it is all tourists, like us, unfortunately. But you can still feel their ghosts. Not just Hemingway, but all of them. Almost that Machu Picchu spiritual sensation they talk about that people feel at the top of the Peruvian mountain. Scary fun. And this was just half of our Hemingway journey. But it was enough for today. We reopened our umbrellas and fought our way back home in the rapidly approaching darkness through the now sideways, screaming Paris rain.

The next day, late morning, we took off to follow Hemingway's ghost in St.-Germain, in the Sixth Arrondissement. We targeted three venerable sites: Les Deux Magots and Café de Flore, almost next to each other on Boulevard St.-Germain, and Brasserie Lipp, directly opposite.

Les Deux Magots calls itself "the Rendezvous of the Intellectual Elite": a bright, upbeat cafe with a long terrace on the boulevard.

Its small street-front tables both indoors and outside are filled from morning till night. Very often, customers will order a coffee and a glass of water and spend the entire morning or afternoon in animated discussions or reading a book or Le Monde. They are left undisturbed. That's just the French way. We wormed our way through the crowd, found a table, and ordered a coffee. We eventually evolved to Champagne on the terrace in the warm sunlight.

Les Deux Magots attracted Hemingway and Joyce, and later the existentialists Sartre, de Beauvoir and Camus. It also attracted the artists Picasso and Léger. Eventually the African-American writers Richard Wright and James Baldwin made it their Paris home away from home, and were often found lost in discussions with Sartre and de Beauvoir. Les Deux Magots, in the spirit of the ethos of their clients, has issued a literary prize to an aspiring young writer since 1933.

Crowds frequently moved between Les Deux Magots and Café de Flore. Sartre and de Beauvoir were different, however. It is said that they would often spend from 9 a.m. until after dinner at Café de Flore. They also did almost all of their writing there. Sartre published "Being and Nothingness" and "No Exit" and de Beauvoir published her first novel, "She Came to Stay," all written there. Every year, the café also awards a literary prize to an up-and-coming writer. This is such an admirable and inspiring French tradition.

Brasserie Lipp, directly across the four-lane boulevard, is a very traditional brasserie with waiters in black waistcoats, bow ties and long white aprons. Almost the exact mental picture you envision in caricatures of French brasseries. Its Art Deco interior and traditional Parisian comfort food attracted French presidents from de Gaulle to Pompidou, Mitterrand and Chirac. Writers including André Gide, André Malraux and Marcel Proust ate here, as well as Hemingway. We sat on their terrace and had a dozen cold, briny oysters with vinaigrette and two glasses of Sancerre and continued our Parisian people-watching on the stylish Boulevard St.-Germain. The waiters were appropriately rude in the spirit of Old Paris. (Actually, most

Parisian waiters are very polite and helpful. Maybe these waiters thought it was part of their Old Paris mystique, like New York Jewish deli waiters.) This is another alluring place that has changed very little in the last 70 years.

There were other interesting Hemingway haunts we visited. The restaurant Polidor, near the Sorbonne, was featured in Woody Allen's film "Midnight in Paris." It likewise seemed unchanged. Bar Hemingway at the Ritz hotel preserves the moment in 1944 when the writer declared it "liberated" from the Nazis and ordered Champagne for everyone. Harry's New York Bar was also interesting but couldn't capture Paris in the 1920s, '30s and '40s the way our first discoveries did.

The Hemingway ghost tour was great fun. But it could just as easily have been a Victor Hugo tour, or Marcel Proust, or Émile Zola or James Joyce. The French recorded everything about their lives as well. For me, it was just that Hemingway's time in Paris had intrigued me since I first read "A Movable Feast" in college. But it wasn't just Hemingway who made the tour so captivating. It was the layers of other artistic, literary and intellectual talents that were hidden below the surface. It was another example of the "palimpsest" effect that we first experienced in Rome. The surface was scraped clean and ready to be used again.

That term is also used in architecture and archaeology to denote an object made for one purpose and reused for another. I can't help but think of it in the same way for the Parisian cafés and meeting places that were used again and again by the generations of great artists, literary figures and philosophers who were drawn to the city from all over Europe and America between the 1870s and the 1950s. This wasn't the ghost of Hemingway tour. It was the ghosts of the 80-year history of the writers, artists and philosophers of Paris.

PÈRE LACHAISE: THE DESTINATION CEMETERY

Only in Paris would there be a "destination cemetery." In the United States, there are special places for special people. Arlington National Cemetery just outside Washington is one. The final resting ground for the U.S. military since the Civil War, it covers 624 acres. It is also the home of the Tomb of the Unknown Soldier. An eternal flame sits at the foot of the graves of President John F. Kennedy and Jacqueline Kennedy Onassis. Senators Robert F. Kennedy and Edward M. Kennedy are interred nearby. A truly historic place.

Paris's greatest memorial has a very different focus. Its largest cemetery spreads over 110 acres of sloping tree-filled grounds and is the final resting place of many of its most famous figures. Not generals or other military men, but 70,000 burial plots and statues of composers, writers, artists, architects, dancers and singers. Each year, Père Lachaise Cemetery has more than 3.5 million visitors, making it the most visited cemetery in the world.

It has been estimated that one million people have been buried there to date. There is now a waiting list, and very few plots are available. Some family mausoleums or multifamily tombs contain dozens of bodies.

We arrived by taxi and entered the main gate, and had walked no more than a hundred yards when an old man with weathered skin, longish gray hair and a tired suit and tie approached us from behind a massive tombstone. He spoke first in French, and when we looked puzzled, he switched to broken English. He explained that he was a cemetery tour guide. He asked us whose tomb we wanted to see. We told him we had a map of the cemetery and didn't need help. He kept repeating Rossini, Rossini, and nodding his head. We responded affirmatively. He took us on a long, convoluted journey in the opposite direction from what the map indicated. We finally ditched him behind a tombstone, spun around and walked away briskly.

Just then, another old, disheveled tour guide appeared from behind another massive gravestone and waved for us to follow him. We declined. Two more appeared from nowhere. For a second, I thought we were in an episode of "The X-Files." Where were Fox Mulder and Dana Scully when we needed them? Lisa just burst out laughing every time a new one appeared.

As we explored the extensive grounds of the cemetery, we were amazed by the large, elaborate and sometimes elegant memorials. We visited the writers Proust, Molière, Balzac and America's Richard Wright. The composer Chopin's tomb was enormous, as were Bizet's gravesite and Rossini's. Eugène Delacroix's tomb was powerful. Gertrude Stein and Alice B. Toklas attracted a crowd. Oscar Wilde drew yet another crowd. We found that Edith Piaf and Isadora Duncan had simple graves. The biggest surprise was an American's grave. The rock singer Jim Morrison's large, flat gravestone and the entire plot were covered in a mountain of flowers. Morrison had, far and away, attracted the biggest crowd of the day. Amazing. Why?

The French psyche is very different from that of their American brothers, and their heroes different from ours. God bless the French. We can learn a lot from them. If we listen.

Bars in Paris

Paris bars are different from one arrondissement to the next. We spent most of our time in the Sixth and Fifth Arrondissements, St. Germain-des-Prés and the Latin Quarter. Because that is where most of the universities are, and therefore many of the students, the area was always high-energy, happening and crowded. Even though the French are more reserved than the Italians, if you have an extroverted wife, the distance is narrowed significantly.

There is a wide range of wonderful bars in Paris. Always experimenting, we went to many of them. We went to bars in dungeons, bars in scary caves filled with bones, Goth bars, swing jazz dance bars, French sports bars, even a bar dedicated to the Green Bay Packers football team. A bit unusual. In the end, we spent most of our time in just three.

The first was Café Laurent, located in the Hotel D'Aubusson. Established in 1690, it has remained a hotspot of literary and artistic life. First host to Rousseau, Voltaire and Montesquieu, and then later Sartre, de Beauvoir and Camus, this jazz club features singers and musicians five days a week. Our tuxedoed bartenders offered expert customer service, advice on restaurants, and directions to other unique bars in the area. Excellent foie gras and toast. When we were unsure what to do, this was always our destination.

Our second was the mysterious Compagnie des Vins Surnaturels. No sign. Obscured windows and door. A desire to remain mysterious. Inside, cozy and romantic. Comfortable chairs and couches. Excellent wine list, great Spanish ham, burrata, and seafood appetizers. Great staff who went out of their way to get to know us and make us feel welcome every time we were there. Special place.

Our third favorite place was a kind of high-class French tapas restaurant, Freddy's. Owned by the owner of our favorite wine store, Freddy's has no phone number, so don't ask. Local crowd, always busy, fun, simple food. Between 7 and 11 at night, forget about getting in. Friendly bartenders from all over Europe made us feel special and like locals.

Of special note, if you can find it, is Le Piano Vache, in the Latin Quarter. This place has the most incredible Spanish jazz guitarist of all time. Students get there early on Mondays to squeeze in to see this amazing performer. Watch his fingers. On both hands. Mesmerizing. Worth the trip from any part of Paris.

In Paris bars, the patrons dress more formally than in Rome. They are more reserved. Quieter. They appear to go out in small groups but otherwise keep to themselves. They set a very different emotional tone from that of Romans or other Italians. Come to think of it, most of the people we developed relationships with were from all over Europe, including Germany, Portugal, Sweden, Denmark, and also the United States. Few were French nationals.

Planning the Last Leg
of the Adventure

Our last three months away would be a trip through Russia, Belarus and Ukraine. My grandparents on my mother's side were Belorussian and Ukrainian immigrants. They were both peasant farmers back then. They emigrated to the United States because of the Russian Civil War between the Red and White Armies. My grandfather was conscripted into the White Army and left Belorussia to avoid the war. My grandmother fled because of the Ukrainian-Soviet War and the invasion of the Bolsheviks. I had wanted to take this trip since I was a small boy and heard their stories, but in those days it was still under the iron hand of the Soviet Union.

We would start this leg of our adventure in St. Petersburg. Founded by Czar Peter the Great in 1703, it was the center of the Russian monarchies and Russian culture for centuries. It has one of the world's greatest collections of Baroque and Neoclassical architecture, including the Winter Palace, the residence of the emperors, and the Hermitage, the second-largest art museum in the world, after the Louvre, with over three million items.

We would then take a 13-day Viking River Cruise called "Waterways of the Tsars." We would travel down the Volga and Svir Rivers and through the expansive Lakes Onega and Ladoga. We would stop at a series of Russian towns and cities along the way, including Uglich and Yaroslavl with their impressive green-domed Russian Orthodox churches and colorful food markets. We had the paperwork for our Russian visas, and Viking River Cruises would be our sponsor.

We would then spend a few weeks in Moscow, the largest city entirely on the European continent. I was always fascinated by Red Square, the Kremlin, the onion domes of St. Basil's Cathedral and the Cathedral of Christ the Savior. Many of these wonderful Moscow buildings were built by Italian architects, some as far back as the Renaissance.

We would then travel to Minsk, where my grandfather was from. It is the capital and largest city of Belarus. It had been part of the Grand Duchy of Lithuania and the Kingdom of Poland, as had much of western Ukraine. It was flattened in World War II and 80 percent of its buildings were destroyed. Now it has a number of attractive museums and galleries, as well as the beautiful St. Mary Magdalene Orthodox Church.

From there we would spend time in Kiev, Ukraine, one of the oldest cities in Eastern Europe and a very important cultural center. It was an influential Christian center in the Russian Empire and an early home of the Russian Orthodox Church. St. Sophia's Cathedral there dates from the 11th century.

Next, we would head to a city on the Polish border called Lviv, where my grandmother was born. Once the capital of the kingdom of Galicia-Volhynia, it is a center of art, literature, opera and theater in western Ukraine, with over 60 museums and a number of theaters.

Aside from the river cruise, we were going to use only hotels on this entire leg and travel only by train.

Lisa was a bit anxious about the trip because of fighting in the Donbass eastern region of Ukraine between Ukrainian troops and Russian paramilitary forces. I tried to ease her concerns by explaining that Kiev was far to the west and unaffected. She remained troubled.

We were in Rome when we and our friends there were shocked to learn that Donald Trump had won the presidential election against all odds. Actually, the next evening when we returned to the Communist Bar, our friends Diego and Paulo grabbed us, moaning, "Joe and Lisa, what did you do? Trump is worse than Silvio Berlusconi! He could be the next Mussolini!" We got the same reaction in our gym and again in the restaurant below our Airbnb. "Joe and Lisa, how could you let this happen?" We had voted before we left via absentee ballots, but we were startled at how closely our European friends were following this news.

We were equally shocked to find out that the intelligence community confirmed that the Russians had intended to interfere in the presidential election. Then on Dec. 29, President Obama expanded sanctions against Russia, expelled 35 Russian diplomats and locked down two Russian diplomatic compounds. The tension between the United States and Russia increased dramatically. That event eliminated the Russian leg of the trip for Lisa. She thought it was just too dangerous at that moment in time.

I immediately began re-planning the final leg of our trip around Istanbul and Turkey. I had briefly been to Istanbul on business and found it fascinating. My time there was just too short, though. Istanbul, historically known as Byzantium, had a big influence on Rome, Venice and the Roman Catholic Church. We could make all of those connections from our education in Italy. Istanbul was the home of the Ottoman Empire, the spellbinding glory of the Hagia Sophia museum and the Blue Mosque.

On New Year's Day, our first day in Paris, a terrorist bombing in the Reina nightclub in the Ortakoy neighborhood of Istanbul killed 39 people and wounded 70. Earlier, on June 29, a series of deadly explosions in the Istanbul Ataturk airport had left 41 dead and 239 wounded. As a result of these two events, Lisa declared that Turkey was now off our list as well.

We had to begin our planning anew. I had brought books on Russia, Belarus and Ukraine to help us navigate the trip. I had read "Natasha's Dance: A Cultural History of Russia." I had been to Turkey before and had a good idea how to shape the details. Now we were flying blind.

AMSTERDAM

Amsterdam was our first side trip from Paris. It was a short (3 hour, 17 minute), pleasant train ride to Amsterdam Centraal Station. We were very excited to visit the city of canals, windmills, museums, bicycles, tulips and our most important priority, legal marijuana.

I had tried marijuana in college and used it the first few years after I graduated, but the legal implications eliminated my continued use of it like many of my generation. Lisa had never tried it. Fifty-eight years old and never tried it. That would be part of our Amsterdam mission: to get Lisa high once.

Amsterdam separated soft drugs from hard drugs, and in the 1970s legalized marijuana as a soft drug. This makes it a destination city for youth from throughout Europe and the United States. There are over 250 coffee shops in the city that sell marijuana, hashish and edible cannabis products like brownies, pound cakes, cookies and even gummy bears. You can buy a book, "Coffeeshop Guide Amsterdam," that reviews coffee houses, and you can also buy a big fold-out map of the city that locates all of them. Every neighborhood. We bought them both.

We decided our Amsterdam itinerary would include one full day touring the canals by boat, and another in the city's two extraordinary museums, the Rijksmuseum, which holds the largest and most important collection of Dutch art, and the Van Gogh Museum. And then we would spend three days exploring the coffee shops and Amsterdam's funky and down-home restaurants. That seemed like a balanced allocation of time.

When we arrived, we discovered why Amsterdam is known as "Venice of the North." There are over 165 canals, 1,200 bridges (three times more than in Venice), 60 miles of waterways and 2,500 houseboats. Amazing.

On our train ride we had read that the 17th century was considered Amsterdam's "golden age." Amsterdam had become the wealthiest city in the Western world. It had created a worldwide trading network that reached Africa, North America, Brazil, Indonesia, India and beyond. It had the largest maritime force in the world. The city was a sea of masts. It was Europe's most important point for the shipment of goods and was the leading financial center in Western Europe. The Dutch West India Company and the Dutch East India Company were the largest trading companies in the world at that time. Wow.

As we had seen in Florence and Venice, and later in Paris, this financial dominance allowed the Dutch to rebuild Amsterdam into a world-class metropolis and, like their predecessors in Florence and Venice, to become major patrons of the arts.

It allowed them to make a comprehensive plan to redesign the city around four major concentric half-circles of canals. The project started in 1613 and was known as the Grachtengordel, or Canal Ring. The three inner canals were targeted for major residential development for the city's newly affluent. They were the Herengracht (Canal of the Lords), Keizersgracht (Emperor's Canal) and Prinsengracht (Prince's Canal). The fourth and outermost canal is the Singelgracht. Both ends of all of the canals connect to the IJ bay, which ultimately opens to the North Sea. It is this marvelous system of city planning, these wonderful sweeping canals, and the extraordinary new homes in the baroque style that were built side-by-side along their banks that make Amsterdam a magical place to live.

The 17th century was also the Dutch golden age of painting. This borrowed from Italian Renaissance and baroque styles but differed in the subject matter. The painting of religious subjects declined sharply. Dutch Calvinism forbade religious painting in churches. The Dutch created whole new genres of painting. They focused on painting in a new Dutch Realist style that featured portraits and genre scenes (scenes from everyday life, like landscapes, seascapes and ships, and still lifes). Enormous quantities of art were produced, over 1.3 million paintings in the 1640s and 1650s alone. It was estimated that 25 percent of the citizens of Amsterdam had a painting in their homes. This age produced two of the greatest artists in the history of Western art: Rembrandt van Rijn and Johannes Vermeer. True masters.

The Rijksmuseum is considered the temple of Dutch painting. It houses the greatest collection of Rembrandt's work, including his breathtaking "Night Watch" as well as the greatest collections of Vermeer, including the magical hyper-real "Milkmaid."

Next to the Rijksmuseum is the equally fascinating Van Gogh Museum. It contains over 200 of his paintings and 580 of his drawings, including a great number of self-portraits and many of his most famous works like "The Sunflowers" and "The Irises." Between them, you leave culturally energized.

Over the week, we wandered the canals every day. Seas of bicycle riders weaved around us. There are an estimated 880,000 bicycles in the city, four times the number of cars. The simple bikes, traveling fast, ringing their bells and honking their horns, were everywhere. The riders weaving this way and that were confident and capable, but you had to always be on the lookout and be careful where and when you changed direction or tried to cross the street so there were no surprises.

We learned the best way to see all of the canals was actually on a boat cruise. Boats pick up and drop off at every major point in the city. At our hotel, the Pulitzer Amsterdam, we found something special: the hotel's "salon boat." A long, thin, 12-person, polished teak and brass, marble and leather cruising boat built in 1909, it picked us up in front of the hotel along the Prinsengracht canal. A guide described the history of the city and the famous homes that lined the canals. We brought along a bottle of Champagne to make it even more special. That's the way to see Amsterdam, from the water. It was splendid.

Our coffee house tour was a blast. Lisa had never liked the idea of smoking, so it was just edibles for her. I tried their pre-rolled joints because I didn't remember how to do it. Actually, I never did it well.

The first day we went to a place called Amnesia Haze, and she had a cookie but nothing happened. The owner told us sometimes that happens your first time. I got very high. Next day we visited a place called AK-47, and Lisa had a piece of pound cake; nothing happened. I got very high again. She was getting depressed that she finally had the courage and conviction to investigate cannabis, but to no effect. The next day we went to the Purple Wreck, the White Widow and the Super Skunk. She had a brownie. Nothing. I got very, very high. Later that evening, we were in an Italian restaurant, and out of the blue, it hit her. It really hit her.

The restaurant started spinning around her and she jumped up awkwardly and almost knocked everything off our table. She said far too loudly that we must leave immediately and head back to our hotel. She attracted everyone's attention. We paid, left, and wandered out into in the Amsterdam darkness. I held her tightly as she weaved back and forth, taking baby steps along the way. It took us 30 minutes to go two blocks. She said we needed to walk very close to the houses to avoid falling into the canal. The canal was 15 feet away. We reached our hotel and Lisa crawled upstairs and went straight to the bed. She sat on the bed for 20 minutes and then demanded I walk her to the bathroom, which was three feet away. I started laughing hysterically. Pot sometimes does that to you. A 10-minute journey with her walking hand-over-hand on the wall got her there on her own.

One and done. Our Amsterdam cannabis adventure was over.

The next morning when we boarded our train to return to Paris, we reminisced about how much we had loved our Venice of the North. The endless, looping canals. The Champagne boat adventure. The splendid museums of Dutch Masters. The manic army of bicyclists. Even the edibles.

'Nice la Belle'

" Nice la Belle." Nice the Beautiful. Lisa and I had vacationed here every year for the last five years. Lisa's sister Ellen and her husband, Daniel, own a wonderful 11th-floor, three-bedroom condo in a fascinating complex on the edge of the Mediterranean. It is in the Port Marina Baie des Anges, the "Bay of Angels," located between Nice and Antibes. The complex is a luxurious residential resort. Its construction began in 1960 and took almost 25 years to complete. It is a 40-acre complex that includes a marina and four giant pyramid-shaped buildings that look like huge waves 70 meters high. We would stay here for a week each summer. Our vacation was focused on pure relaxation. Swimming and sunning at the pool. Swimming in the Mediterranean. Occasional side trips to great restaurants in the mountaintop village of Èze, or the wonderful seaside seafood restaurant Le Bacon, in Antibes. Or we would just wander the marina and eat casually in one of the many simple seafood or Italian restaurants. Those vacations were purely to chill from the stress of work.

This time it would be different. Same condo but different lens. We would search out the art of the Impressionists, Post-Impressionists, Fauvists, Cubists, Surrealists and Modernists. Cézanne, Renoir, Matisse, van Gogh, Léger, Giacometti, Picasso and Chagall.

Paul Cézanne started the migration of Impressionist and Post-Impressionist artists from Paris to the warm, sunny, bright, beautiful, deep blue Côte d'Azur. He returned from Paris to his hometown of Aix-en-Provence in the 1880s to paint in solitude. It was here in the South of France that he revolutionized painting once again with his still lifes, portraits, landscapes and studies of bathers. It was here that he painted the view of Mont Ste.-Victoire. These mountain landscapes, which he painted continuously over an eight-year period, depicted planes of blues and greens forming complex fields of color. They are breakthroughs in painting, and works for which he is most renowned. He painted over 130 versions of that mountain over those years. Picasso referred to Cézanne as "the father of us all" and claimed him as "my one and only master."

We bought a monthly ticket for unlimited use on the local train that traces the coastline from Nice to Cannes, with stops at Cagnes-sur-Mer, Villeneuve-Loubet, Biot, Antibes and Juan-les-Pins along the way. These were some of the towns to which the artists migrated from Paris to capture the beauty and the mesmerizing blues and greens of the Côte d'Azur.

Matisse lived and worked in Nice from 1917 to 1954 in an apartment studio at the Hotel Regina. The Matisse Museum in Nice houses one of the world's greatest collections of his work, tracing his entire career. The museum has 68 paintings and gouaches, 236 drawings, 218 prints, 95 photos, 57 sculptures and 14 books illustrated by the artist. His use of solid colors drove him to the leadership of the Fauvist movement.

Nearby is the Musée National Marc Chagall, which has the largest collection of that artist's work. It houses an amazing series of 17 paintings illustrating the biblical message of the books of Genesis, Exodus and the Song of Songs. The enormous size, bright colors, complexity of hidden biblical messages, and sheer overwhelming beauty of these works take your breath away. The museum holds over 400 paintings, gouaches, drawings and wash drawings, as well as breathtaking stained glass. Chagall lived his final years in nearby St.-Paul-de-Vence, working on new projects until his death at 97.

A quick taxi ride along steep, winding roads took us to that lovely old mountaintop village. At the foot of the village's 16th-century walls sits the famous La Colombe d'Or restaurant and hotel. Originally a café bar with an open-air terrace, it reopened as an inn with three bedrooms. It soon became the meeting place of internationally known artists such as Picasso, Miró, Braque, Léger and Chagall. When they came together, they paid for their meals "in kind," in the form of paintings and sculptures instead of money. These works adorn the walls of the restaurant and hotel to this day. In 1951 Yves Montand and Simone Signoret were married here.

The Maeght Foundation, a short, steep walk up the road from the restaurant, houses one of the biggest collections of 20th-century art in Europe. It includes works by Braque, Calder, Chagall, Giacometti, Kandinsky, Léger, Miró and others. The collection contains 12,000 pieces of art in all media, and is surrounded by a sculpture park displaying many magnificent works.

A short train ride took us to the town of Antibes. On the marina there is the imposing, two-story stone Picasso Museum, which occupies the former Château Grimaldi. Picasso spent 1946 in Antibes, using the second floor of this castle as his workshop. It became the first museum to be dedicated to the artist. Today it holds 245 works by Picasso. His paintings were inspired by the marine and mythological life of the Mediterranean. The museum also displays some of his most significant ceramic works created in his Vallauris studio. The terrace of the castle offers a permanent collection of remarkable sculptures by Miró and others.

In the seaside village of Biot, another short trip by train, is the Fernand Léger National Museum. It is a unique collection of over 450 paintings, ceramics and drawings displayed chronologically, which reflect the history of his colorful cubist compositions. It is on the site of his villa, the farmhouse St. Andrew, at the foot of the village where he died in 1955. The museum was built under the patronage of Picasso, Braque and Chagall. Monumental mosaics created by Léger cover three sides of this unique building, including a 5,000-square-foot mosaic on the front facade.

A short walk from our condo, through the nearby village of Cagnes-sur-Mer, is the home and studio of the famous French Impressionist Auguste Renoir. The Renoir Museum of

Cagnes-sur-Mer or Domaine des Collettes sprawls over seven acres in an olive grove. The artist worked there until his death in 1919. Matisse, Modigliani, Rodin, Picasso and Monet were frequent guests, and the museum contains works by many of his old friends.

Our visit to Nice wasn't all museums. We interspersed leisurely strolls through Old Nice, the old town of Antibes, the village of St.-Paul-de-Vence, and Nice's Roman ruins.

The most fun we had that wondrous month was visiting the plages – the beaches of Nice, Juan-les-Pins and Cannes. They set a high bar for excellence with row upon row of beachfront umbrellas just feet from the beautiful blue Mediterranean. Restaurants there serve excellent French food, with an emphasis on fresh seafood. Many are extensions of their five-star parent hotels across the street from the beach. They line the exclusive Croisette in Cannes and the equally exclusive Promenade des Anglais in Nice. If you get the chance, try the Carlton Plage and Miramar Plage in Cannes and the Castel Plage and Plage Beau Rivage restaurants in Nice. Unforgettable relaxing afternoons on the breezy beach. Great music as well.

So Nice isn't just sun and relaxation after all. For us it turned out to be the perfect continuation of our exploration of Western art. And a great one.

THE CHÂTEAUNEUF–DU–PAPE WINE TOUR

While we were in Europe, we gave ourselves room to change our plans whenever we had an epiphany or a sudden passion to explore something we hadn't thought of before. That was part of the fun of it. It kept things always exciting and new.

A wine tour of the Châteauneuf-du-Pape region was one of those epiphanies. Many Americans have some knowledge of the Bordeaux and Burgundy regions, as they are among the most popular in France, but the Châteauneuf-du-Pape region, in the Rhône Valley of France's southeast, operated under the radar for years. In the 1970s, though, the influential wine critic Robert Parker raised its profile from that of an afterthought in French wine to being considered the most undervalued and underappreciated, and declared it the greatest price-value relationship in all of France. He even scored a number of its wines a 100, his highest ranking, normally reserved for the best-of-the-best of Bordeaux wine like Château Lafite Rothschild, Château Haut-Brion and Château Margaux, which can sell for $1,000 to $2,500 a bottle when ranked 100 points. Even the Châteauneuf-du-Pape winemakers themselves give Parker the credit for this meteoric rise in their popularity. He has always been my favorite wine critic, and we decided that we must make a trip there happen.

It was May and we were in Barcelona. We would plan the trip two months out when we would be in Nice, a reasonable train ride away. I researched tour guides on the internet, and found one that looked great, Rhône Wine Tours. They had six major potential tours of the Rhône region, and two would fit our plan. The most exciting was an "all-inclusive wine holiday" covering both the northern Rhône and the southern Rhône regions where the Châteauneuf-du-Pape grapes are grown. It was expensive at $1,000 per person for five days, but it included hotels and meals. We would go for it.

When we finally reached them we were disappointed that the tour had already sold out. We would take our second choice, Big Reds of the South. Also sold out. O.K., we would book the "bespoke" wine tour of the south for just the two of us. Sorry, all guides were booked for the entire season. Damn. But they told us about a woman with her own small business and said she was very good. They gave us her name, Sophie Bergeron, her website, travelinprovence.net, and her telephone number. We were disappointed but decided to give it a try.

On her website we learned that Sophie had gone to university in Avignon, Montpellier and London and received a master's and Ph.D. in English and a degree in international business with a specialization in wine. She had worked for three years at one of Châteauneuf-du-Pape's top vineyards, Domaine la Janasse. We quickly called and booked her for the third week of July. Wow. We lucked out.

We compiled a list of the best-of-the best Châteauneuf-du-Pape vineyards, and Sophie got us appointments at all except one. The vineyards on our list were rated much higher than our original Rhone Wine Tours choices. Amazing. It turned out she lives in the town of Orange, the center of the region, and she knows everyone. She helped get us a hotel room in town. She booked us at the three best restaurants in the region. This was getting better all the time. Now we were eager to start this exciting journey.

When we arrived at our hotel, the desk clerk told us with great excitement that we were just in time for the final performance of the Chorégies d'Orange at the Théâtre Antique d'Orange. Sorry, Lisa inquired, but what are you talking about? It is the oldest music festival in France, the clerk responded. The performances are in an ancient Roman theater in the center of Orange. A Roman amphitheater? Lisa asked again.

Yes, the young woman explained. Orange was founded by the Romans in 35 B.C., built as a miniature Rome with the theater, a temple complex and a forum. Only the scale of the buildings had been reduced — the theater seats 9,000. The music festival has been held since 1860, and everyone in town is going to tonight's final performance, the clerk said. You do have tickets, don't you? No, Lisa responded, we had never heard of it until you just explained it to us. The clerk said that if we acted fast, maybe we could get tickets from a scalper. She checked us in, gave us our keys and rushed us to our elevator.

She told us how to get there and we took off, walking briskly through the quant old village. In less than five minutes, the massive amphitheater rose into the sky. It was amazingly well-preserved, in better condition than the Roman Colosseum. How had I not noticed this architectural gem in my research? Crowds had already filled all of the nearby outdoor cafés and all the streets in the immediate area. But no scalpers could be found. Though our prospects were dim, we went to the box office. Yes, they had two seats, the most expensive in the theater, naturally. After arguing with each other about the cost, we bought them. Just in time. They were now admitting the crowds. The performance was Beethoven's Ninth Symphony.

Television cameras and floodlights were everywhere on the ground floor of the theater. We climbed up the broad stone steps a third of the way to the top and found our seats. The extroverted Lisa asked our neighbor if she could tell us anything about the theater or the performance. We were in luck; the woman was an opera singer from the United States, and her husband was the tenor soloist in the concert. She took us through the history of the festival, the exceptional acoustics of the theater, its history of performers including Placido Domingo and other famous singers, and the history of operas performed there including "Tosca," "Aida," "Faust" and "Carmen." Wow, how did we fall into this?

The orchestra and the choir were spectacular, and the set design and lighting were as well. The orchestra and the amphitheater were bathed in waves of violet and green light, and spotlights highlighted the choir and singled out the soloists. Her husband was amazing. Tears ran down her face, she was so proud of his performance. Standing ovation after standing ovation. Sometimes amazing things happen to you that you can never foresee. This was one.

The next morning, Sophie Bergeron, our guide, met us in our lobby. As you might imagine, Lisa and she quickly became best friends, discussing children, educational backgrounds, travel, favorite wines, everything under the sun. She drove us to a who's who of Châteauneuf-du-Pape wineries for tastings and education. At Roger Sabon, the owner showed us the 13 different varieties of grapes that make up the wines, including Grenache, Syrah and Mourvèdre. He explained the various types of rocks and soil — limestone, sandstone, red clay, sand and large river rocks — and their effect on the taste of the wine. He explained the "secret" of how he makes his exclusive wine called Secret. Great education and great fun.

We spent lunch at a wonderful restaurant in nearby Gigondas, the Hôtel les Florets, set outdoors on a beautiful flower-filled terrace surrounded by massive trees shading us from the hot sun. We overlooked the vineyards, fields of waving lavender, and the jagged peaks jutting into the sky from the Dentelles de Montmirail, the highest mountains in Provence, in the distance.

At another vineyard, Paul Autard and his daughter took Lisa and me through their processes for harvesting and destemming, the vignification process, and aging in oak barrels vs. the concrete tanks of most of the other local vineyards. He recently made his daughter his marketing manager and he was showing her the ropes.

The next day was wonderful as well. More tastings. Pierre Usseglio, Pegau, Beaucastel, and La Nerthe all told us their stories.

Le Verger des Papes provided another great lunch at another fairy-tale setting. The restaurant is at the top of the hill where a medieval castle was the summer residence of the popes when they were in Avignon. Hence the name Châteauneuf-du-Pape, the pope's new castle. Sitting on a patio next to the high castle walls, we had breathtaking views of the Rhône Valley, the meandering river and the mountains rising beyond. Shaded by pine trees and surrounded by olive and almond trees, it was another dreamlike setting and another wonderful meal.

More tasting the next morning took us to Domaine la Janasse, where Sophie had worked for a number of years. She gave us a private tour and a private tasting of all of their finest wines.

Next, we spent meaningful time with the two sisters who own the vineyard Marcoux. One sister runs the fields, and the other handles production, sales and marketing. They allowed us to do vertical tastings. Lisa and I tasted the same wine from multiple years, and the sisters explained how different conditions — rain, temperatures, the mistral winds — caused the variations in taste. Fascinating.

On this day, lunch was on the patio of the castle-like Château des Fines Roches. From the second-floor outdoor restaurant, we looked out on the estate's rolling hills and vineyards. Large river rocks lay among the vines, and the fields seemed to go on forever. For lunch, we had wonderful foie gras with figs, almond bread, sweetbread confit, and a selection of wonderful local goat cheese. And naturally, a great local wine: Châteauneuf-du-Pape.

Between restaurants and tastings, Sophie walked us through fields to show us how the vineyards were maintained, the different grapes and how they tasted, and much more.

A few more amazing vineyards and tastings and we were done. But not before buying bottles of wine from a number of places that are very difficult to get in the United States, like Clos des Papes and Château de Vaudieu. We would take some to drink in Nice, and some to take home.

We became very close with Sophie. Our lunches were always together. We talked about France, the United States, her time in

London, her son, her husband, Orange and the recent influx of immigrants, and just life in general. Along the way, her relationships with owners got us into vineyards that practically no one gets to visit and allowed us to sample wines that few get the chance to taste. We took countless photos of the three of us together and with the vineyard owners, in the vineyards and from atop the old pope's castle. Today, Lisa writes to Sophie every time something is in the news in France. A forest fire. A terrorist attack. A memorable week gave us a lasting friendship.

AIR, RAIL, AUTO, CAB, METRO OR WALK?

I f you plan to spend a year in Europe, an overall transportation strategy is important. It depends on how you like to travel and how you like to observe and experience things. Lisa and I learned an important lesson years ago on our honeymoon in France. Although she loves to drive and I am very good at navigating, it turns out it just doesn't work out well, being together in a car. So our first important decision was easy. No rental cars.

We love the European rail system, so an early decision was to travel between every major city by rail.

In France, the high-speed train is the TGV (Train à Grande Vitesse), operated by their national network, SNCF. It can reach speeds of 357 miles per hour, and many travel at 200 m.p.h. We took these trains to Lyon, Amsterdam, Orange, Nice and Barcelona. The French trains were always on time. Their only quirky behavior was that the train staff turned a blind eye toward "hitchhikers": students or itinerants who sneaked onto the double-decker trains and kept changing seats, moving between the upper and lower levels and from car to car, and hiding out in restrooms to avoid being checked for tickets. We saw entire families doing it. Obviously first class was their compartment of choice. If you are going to sneak, sneak the best.

In Italy, the high-speed network is the Alta Velocità, and the individual lines are called the Frecciarossa, which offered 72 daily trips nationwide at 220 m.p.h., the Frecciargento, at 155 m.p.h., and the Frecciabianca, which runs at 125 m.p.h. They are all operated by the national rail system, Trenitalia. The trip from Rome to Florence, about 170 miles, was only an hour and 16 minutes. A joy through the beautiful mountain countryside. We traveled with them to Siena, Florence and Venice. The Italian train staff, dressed in jackets and ties, were a little pompous, but the wine they poured was great.

In Spain, it is the AVE, the Alta Velocidad Española, operated by their national network, Renfe. We used it to travel to Seville and Cordoba.

They were all incredible experiences. If you plan enough in advance, there are always sales on first-class tickets, and the accommodations were spacious and very comfortable and often included wine and gracious service. We sometimes brought our own wine, baguettes, cheeses, Spanish hams and other fun snacks, to the dismay of our fellow passengers. We would always vote for traveling by rail.

By the end, we had made more than 40 train trips. Roma Termini, Gare de Lyon, Gare du Nord, Barcelona Sants, Amsterdam Centraal, Santa Maria Novella – it was all a blur. But compared with air travel, it was a blessing. No rush to the airport. Always a short trip across town. No baggage check. No check-in lines. No bus to the plane. No changing terminals. And beautiful cross-country vistas, mountain ranges, forests, vineyards, farmers, horses. Postcard-worthy journeys.

Traveling within a city, we had a similar set of choices. Should we always use the metro?

The Paris Métro is the second-busiest subway system in Europe, after Moscow. It has 16 lines, and many of its 303 stations are done in a beautiful Art Nouveau style. The Rome Metro is much smaller. It has been cautious in its expansion because of fear of disrupting ancient Roman ruins. In between in size is the Barcelona Metro, which has taken some very modern approaches with operations, including driverless vehicles.

At the end of the day, we thought long and hard about the metros but selected almost 100 percent walking and a very limited use of taxis. We chose Airbnb locations in the center of the city, which almost always allowed us to get everywhere by foot.

In Paris, we planned to spend most of our time in just the central seven of its 20 arrondissements. We selected St.-Germain-des-Prés, in the Sixth Arrondissement on the Left Bank, to live in, bordering the Fifth and Seventh Arrondissements and across the Seine from the First, Second, Third and Fourth. This is the beautiful heart of Paris, home to its attractions, restaurants and clubs. We passed the glorious Notre-Dame and the magnificent Louvre multiple times a day. We walked along the Seine and across its many bridges just as often. Found exciting art galleries down little side streets. Discovered underground music clubs down alleyways. The strategy worked. We took two taxis in three months.

The strategy was the same in Rome. Almost the exact center of the city. Passed the Pantheon constantly, as well as the Piazza Navona's amazing Bernini fountain sculptures and the flowers and fruit stalls of the Campo de' Fiori. Discovered the city's most amazing coffee company and gelato shop. Wonderful art galleries. It worked again. We needed only four taxis in three months to get us to attractions that were a bit out of our range.

And the same was true in Barcelona. On the south side of the city near the waterfront, between the Gothic Quarter and El Born and directly across from Port Vell and the beach neighborhood of the Barceloneta, we could get almost anywhere easily. We wandered the beaches and the little backstreet tapas cafés and funky student bars in the Barceloneta, El Born and the Gothic Quarter every day. Three taxis in three months.

The walking strategy was a glorious success. We gained no weight. We probably saw more than any American tourist who had ever visited those towns. We probably saw as much as the average resident sees in a lifetime. Different streets and routes every day, surprises everywhere, always a new discovery. And the most startling

BARCELONA

We arrived at the Barcelona Sants railway station in a downpour. It was rattling the roof of the station. We dragged our too, too many bags on our multiple carts through the busy station out onto the covered outside curb. We could only see two feet ahead of us in the pouring rain. We followed the signs down the long walkway to the taxis. We had been told by our host that it would be a simple ride to the Airbnb. We would need two taxis because of all of our bags. I had a feeling this was going to be a bad idea. Why did we let ourselves be talked out of ordering a large van? Simple? Damn.

The taxis stood just out of range to reach comfortably in this Shakespearean "Tempest"-like storm. They were five feet from the curb and the covered walkway, and I had a strange feeling that the taxi drivers weren't planning to get out to help us get our luggage into the cabs. I was right. We procrastinated for what seemed like forever and, in a mad, comic dash, ran for the taxis dragging our overfilled carts. We almost drowned trying to jam all of our things into the two cars.

Lisa and I both had the address on the back of business cards that we handed to the drivers, but we had no idea where we were going and what would it look like when we arrived. There was also the problem of the language. Our drivers spoke Catalan, the language of northeast Spain. No English. We just hoped our directions were foolproof. Lisa's car took off and quickly lost my cab. These guys could take us to Gibraltar and we wouldn't know. After a 30-minute drive through the blinding storm, we stopped. The driver pointed at a narrow five-story building with balconies. It looked like the picture.

Lisa was huddled in the small entranceway, soaked. She looked lost. I opened the cab door and the street was literally flooded. A stream was carrying everything in its path toward the nearby harbor.

Now the cabdriver helped me. He helped unload everything I had into the swirling stream around us. The water was rising up the side of my bags. I paid him and he quickly disappeared. Lisa rushed over to help stack my things, bag by bag, into a big pile in the doorway. What a mess. The ground floor of this building was a restaurant. A waiter had been assigned to check us in. He also spoke no English. When we asked for the owner he nodded, went into the back to get our keys, and helped us drag our bags up to the elevator and eventually into our third-floor unit. He smiled at us and left.

We sat there depressed. We had left the dark, overcast winter months of Paris for a dream apartment in a mild, Mediterranean climate. We had expected 70-degree days with sunlight lifting us into the heavens. What happened?

And then the rain stopped. And the storm clouds were pushed out to sea. And the sun did appear radiantly from behind the last cloud. We went over to the 15-foot-high, four-foot-wide oak and glass double doors that led to our third-floor porch. A glorious view emerged. We looked directly out onto Port Vell, Barcelona's beautiful main harbor, packed with massive 250-foot superyachts and sailboats. It is the home of the Royal Nautical Club of Barcelona, as well as one of Europe's largest aquariums. And just beyond the port were the beautiful white sands of Barcelona's Mediterranean beaches. The entire area was redesigned and rebuilt in support of the visitors for the 1992 Barcelona Olympics.

We were separated from the port by a beautiful square and, to our right, the massive Catalan-Modernist Central Barcelona Post Office, built in 1927. Four soaring columns support enormous statues that in turn are topped by a coat of arms. It's both a museum and a functioning post office. We gazed onto what must be the most beautiful view in the city. We would grow to love this place. And it didn't rain again for a long time.

Our Airbnb apartment was wonderful as well. A first. The two-story flat was designed by the architect husband of the restaurateur on the ground floor. It had 30-foot ceilings in the living room and dining room and a long set of riserless stairs that took us up to the master bedroom. The bathrooms and showers were modern and unique. An office overlooked the first floor through a glass panel. And everything worked, including the Wi-Fi. A first. The restaurant owner also manages a farm where she lives. She brought us fresh fruit and vegetables. It gave us new faith in the Airbnb network and its members.

After unpacking, we had to see the city. We walked down the main highway to the beach. Superyachts wall-to-wall docked at the port on one side, with wall-to-wall seafood and tapas restaurants on the other. The most significant thing, though, was a feeling of freedom, joie de vivre, and just plain fun. Lots of young people, and older locals walking in groups. College students out with their friends. Almost no tourist buses, no guides holding flags or umbrellas leading people in silent marches. It was as if everyone here had come to just live life and enjoy. This part of town is called La Barceloneta. It used to be the old fishermen's neighborhood but was dramatically changed in the 1992 Olympic rebuild.

We reached the beach in 20 minutes. Everyone was laughing, talking, filling the inexpensive open-air beachfront bars and restaurants with their friends. It was the Jersey Shore without the Jersey. We walked farther down the beach and discovered two block-long gym and beach clubs where, we learned, Spain's Olympic water polo teams and swimmers trained. The beach stretches half the length of the city from the distinctive Hotel W at one end of the waterfront to the great clubs and restaurants built around the Olympic Village on the other. People walk that stretch every day, watching the paddle-boarders, day-sailors, wet-suited surfers and one another, stopping for the occasional cava along the way.

We joined those gyms and walked there every day to work out. Run, lift and swim. Walk the beach. Fit in one interesting museum in the afternoon. Return for tapas-hopping many nights. There are a lot of interesting and fun sections of Barcelona, but La Barceloneta is its heart.

As we drifted home along the main boulevard, we spied an exquisite "private club" named One Ocean jutting out into Port Vell at the end of a long row of superyachts. It is inside a high fence that keeps the private restaurant just for the people from the exclusive boats. It has a guard in a glass guardhouse, and gates he can raise when a boat owner's automobile approaches. We approached him. He asked in English if we were members of the club. We said we were, and he allowed us in. Victory. We approached the maître d' in the restaurant and asked how one could join the club. She asked us how long we were staying. We responded three months. She gave us some paperwork and asked for our passports. We filled it out, returned it, and she said we were in. Amazing. Who knew?

We walked the perimeter of the restaurant along the water. There were rows of beautiful people, men in their sailing best, suits and ties, and that European look. Beautiful women, very fashionably dressed. Tuxedoed waiters served the outdoor tables and big white umbrellas shaded the diners. They looked out onto the tall masts of the sailboats on one side and the superyachts on the other. The sailboats leaned to and fro with the breeze. Inside was another restaurant, classy and modern. Both restaurants were reservations only. We exited a side door, crossed a small open platform, and entered an upscale bar with tables and intimate booths facing the sailboats on its opposite side.

We took two seats at the bar and were warmly greeted by the bartender, José. He is small, wiry, dark-skinned and handsome, with a huge head of curly hair that is somewhere between Larry from the Three Stooges and Albert Einstein. Lisa's extroverted self emerged and soon we knew everything about José. He came from Venezuela originally. He lives with his girlfriend, who has a small child. He gets high every day after work. Everything. Then she got to know José Maria, the woman who managed the bar: late 20s, tall, very attractive, auburn hair, very friendly, always kidding around and laughing, and always very well-dressed in the latest Spanish fashions. She is a local, single, and into Barcelona's nightclub scene. Then Lisa met Basam, the Palestinian waiter, who is the practical joker of the bunch. He has a crazy, wiry head of hair that rivals José's, only his is more like Groucho Marx. He has a Swedish girlfriend. Lisa also made friends with Eric, the other bartender, who is from Colombia and whose specialty is unique mojitos and margaritas. He is serious and quiet. Within an hour, we had built another family, much like our downstairs bar and restaurant family at our Airbnb and our Communist Bar family in Rome.

This would become our go-to family in Barcelona. Over time, they educated us about the best standing-room-only, crazy, packed, high-energy Champagne, cava and tapas specialty restaurants in town. When and where unique local Catalonian events were occurring, like the return of the fisherman festival in La Barceloneta. The best local wine store. The best cool Spanish clothing. They would become the guides of our local experiences. The anchors of our time in Barcelona. It was a fantastic start.

SUPERMARKETS IN EUROPE

S upermercato. Supermarché. Supermercado. In Europe everyone walks to the supermarket. People in large American cities do that too, but most of us live in suburban or rural communities. We take our car, use a shopping cart, push the cart to our car when we're finished, and drive home.

In Europe, you will surely need to walk home with your food and supplies, even if it's just a few blocks. The first thing you need to do is buy one of those lightweight folding shopping carts, sometimes called a "trolley dolly." You know, the ones you see old ladies pulling around. Or sometimes homeless people.

Trust me. After avoiding tendinitis in both elbows, you will thank me for this simple advice. It is the only way to survive. You can get an inexpensive one for 15 or 20 euros, and it's well worth it.

Even with our routine of eating just one real meal each day, we still needed things at the store. We bought coffee, sweetener, wine, sparkling water, paper goods, and cheese. Besides, supermarkets are an education — and everybody goes there.

Supermarkets in Italy have an entire aisle dedicated to pastas, and even more sauces. Not a surprise. Same thing in France for cheeses. And in Spain for cheeses and hams. In all of them, we avoided the prepared foods aisle. We could never be sure when they had been prepared.

Also, avoid a country's specialty foods in a grocery store, like the top French, Spanish and Italian cheeses, French foie gras, and Italian and Spanish hams. Stick to a specialty shop. Bread is pretty safe because it often comes from the supermarket's own bakery or a specialty baker in town. In Paris, however, always go to the boulangerie.

Fish? Go to a dedicated seafood store in Rome or Paris, or in Barcelona, to one of the big markets in every section of town like Mercat de la Boqueria or Mercat de Santa Caterina. For meats, go to a dedicated butcher in Rome, Paris or Barcelona.

The wine available in supermarkets, though, is surprisingly good and inexpensive. Italian, French and Spanish people drink wine at most meals, and they are very knowledgeable about wine and frugal when they buy it. It all adds up to a good selection at very fair prices. White wines are especially good and predictable in quality. You can get a fine white wine for 6 euros. (Please don't tell our wine snob friends in the U.S. that we frequently bought €6 bottles of wine.)

Barcelona has some attractive Carrefours and El Cortes Ingles stores, but the predominating local stores are little Asian-owned groceries on most street corners. Only good for simple things. Ice is good. Wine is fine. Chips and dip. Water. Otherwise stick to the big farmers markets.

Now the things to be careful about. Toilet paper. There is no equivalent to Charmin in Europe. Not even close. You have to shop very carefully. If you don't speak the language, you must look closely at the pictures on the plastic wrapper. If they don't have a baby or a small girl on the wrapper, you must steer clear. Even those can be unforgiving.

Because of the high cost of space in major European cites, supermarkets are often on two or three floors. If you don't see what you are looking for, check for stairs or an elevator. Low-cost paper goods and household items are often in the basement.

The worst thing about European supermarkets is the check-out girls. They all hate their jobs and their customers as well. (Sorry to seem sexist but there are few checkout boys.) These girls are rude. They pretend they don't hear you or don't understand you, even if you try to speak their language.

But first thing, buy that shopping cart. If you don't want to carry it to the next city, buy one in every major city you go to for a month or more. It's a lifesaver.

GYMS IN EUROPE

If you are going to allow yourself unfettered access to Europe's gastronomic wonders, the first thing you need to do in every city is join a gym. Our extraordinary 2½-hour lunches made the gym a necessity. And buying the scale to weigh ourselves. Seriously. Buying the scale back in Rome had required using the Google Translate app on our iPhones to explain to the clerk in the hardware store what we wanted, after a futile 20 minutes gesturing.

We joined gyms in Rome, Florence, Siena, Paris, Lyon, Barcelona, Seville and Nice. Our hotels had gyms in Venice, Amsterdam and Orange. The first thing we did in every new town, after checking in, was join a gym. We looked on the internet to find two to three gyms within walking distance (up to 30 minutes, say) and visited all of them. Checked for ratings and write-in evaluations. In the end, it always worked out very well. We were always happy. We didn't gain any weight over our entire trip. Excellent!

It doesn't matter if you use the elliptical as we did, or the treadmill or the stationary bike. We found that walking even long distances wasn't enough. We used the machines to lift weights as well, but that is your option. It was great for us.

We walked every morning after coffee. Few gyms were especially close. The Rome walk took us past the Pantheon and through the Piazza Navona, squeezing between the tiny produce and seafood trucks delivering to restaurants. Siena took us up and down hills in the misty morning, allowing us to gaze over the beautiful city's majestic cathedrals.

In Paris, the walk took us past the famous Church of St.-Germain-des-Prés, down busy St.-Germain Boulevard, and through the Odéon movie district and the medieval gardens and laughter-filled children's park at the Musée National du Moyen Age. We returned home the back way, past the Sorbonne and its noisy, animated students, through the beautiful Luxembourg Gardens, past Luxembourg Palace (the seat of the French Senate), and around the magnificent Church of St.-Sulpice and its glorious square.

Barcelona took us past the massive yachts in the harbor and along the edge of the beach in the crisp morning. Every walk was a wake-up call to experience the here and now. Sometimes we were the first people out exploring the town.

Our ritual involved carrying our little bags with our iPhones for movies, our headphones, and our towels and gym locks. In Rome, Paris, and Barcelona alike, we became regulars and the staff knew us and welcomed us.

Every city had its own quirks. At the Italian gym, young guys in white sleeveless T-shirts would grunt loudly while lifting, sometimes even roaring. Then Lisa would get on the same machines and have to increase the weights because the men were lifting such light loads.

In Paris, the members had a thing about saving a machine for a friend or spending half the time on each machine texting or talking to friends on the phone.

In Barcelona, we found it unusual that the locker room was such a social affair. Men and women alike would be naked for long periods walking around and laughing, telling boisterous stories across the room, or sitting on the locker room bench and talking to each other with someone's private parts inches from their face.

Our gym in Rome had a wine bar. We would have a Prosecco as a reward on lifting days. The chef and the bartender became our friends. We sang Christmas carols with them in English and then hummed along when they sang in Italian. We went to the club's Christmas party, the only Americans there.

We joined two sporting clubs in Barcelona, Club Natació Atlètic-Barceloneta and Club Natació Barcelona. They are located right next to each other in La Barceloneta neighborhood, on Passeig de Joan de Borbó, the main drag in this part of the city and right at the beach. They are a combination of gyms, competitive swim racing clubs, competitive water polo clubs, racquet clubs and sailing clubs. One has two outdoor lap pools and two indoor lap pools. The other has a total of five pools, including one fed by salt water direct from the Mediterranean. Each club is a city block long. Between them, they supply all of the competitive water polo players for the Spanish Olympic team. They are both also legacy institutions in Barcelona.

We spent our entire morning at one or the other every day. After exercising, we swam laps with the locals. Two to a lane, sometimes three, fun but serious swimming. Then lying around on the deck to get a small amount of morning sun before it got too hot. It was a joy.

You must be thinking, why two clubs? Well, after researching them both, we decided the first one was the more prestigious. Old-money Barcelona aristocracy, that's for us. Well, after the first few weeks, it was clear that "old money" in Barcelona meant "old people." Old, old people. That was fine, but at the pools and the beach lounge sunning areas, old, topless, overly tanned women and Speedo-wearing, stomach-bulging, old men got very "old" very quickly for us. On to club number two. Welcome attractive, high-energy young people.

THE FUNERAL

We returned from Barcelona to Toms River, N.J., to attend Barbara's funeral. Over 80 family members and friends were there. My brother Charlie worked with her parish priest to put the service together. After the Mass, where I delivered her eulogy, we all returned to her home. Her next-door neighbor and best friend, Millie, invited Mom's friends from her painting classes, her regular card game friends, her shuffleboard league friends, her coffee club friends, and her swim club friends. They were all women. All of their husbands had died. They were all about five feet tall and looked like the cast from Munchkin Land from "The Wizard of Oz" as they poured through the front door. They told us great funny stories about Barbara, hugged us and gave us strong emotional support. It was a noisy, crowded, but intimate group in her small home.

My brothers, our children, grandchildren and cousins were there in force. Mom was the last of her generation in both my parents' families. It was a very sad day for all of us. She was a remarkable woman who ensured we stayed close to one another because she felt it was important. Family and extended family.

My mom's lifelong friend Eileen Brosko, who went to high school with her in Kearny, N.J., gave the blessing at Barbara's home. They had been close friends for 75 years. She is an ordained minister with a doctorate in theology. Her speech about Mom's life, their special friendship, and all their years together was very moving. Another cry. For Eileen as well.

My brother Tom and his son, Kyle, put together 10 oversize poster boards on A-frames with hundreds of photos of Barbara's life, with my dad, with my brothers when we were children, with our children, my cousins and her friends, and they even found a photo of her dressed up for Halloween as a gangster from the 1920s with Eileen and a number of other high school girlfriends. It was both heartwarming and melancholic.

My mom's best friend when we were growing up, Rosemary Green, came to help us celebrate the joy of her life. They had been close friends for 54 years. Her husband, Pat, had recently died. Rosemary was the last remaining parent we were aware of who was still alive from our old neighborhood.

Holly, Tom's wife, arranged the catering. It was a great spread. We also bought 40 Italian hotdogs on gigantic torpedo rolls filled with potatoes, onions and peppers — my dad's, my brothers' and cousins' favorites when we were growing up. They disappeared within minutes.

That day was the first time I internalized that Mom was really gone. When you are in your 60s that is an existential moment, the temporality of life. The last family member of her generation. It is such a cliché, but it etches in your soul that you must breathe, experience, live every moment of every day.

It gave even greater clarity and meaning to our European adventure as we headed back to Barcelona.

THE BEST OF BARCELONA:
TAPAS–HOPPING

Barcelona has a wide variety of excellent restaurants, including a number with Michelin stars. Lasarte is perhaps its top restaurant, with excellent local food, and Enoteca Paco Pérez and Moments are excellent as well. Specialties at these unique places range from Peruvian to Japanese. Lisa and I went to many of them and loved them.

There actually are three other types of restaurants that dominate the Barcelona scene. The first is a small group of wonderful seafood restaurants that serve local fresh fish caught daily. Most of these also excel at the city's most famous dish, seafood paella.

The best of these are in the section known as La Barceloneta, where Barcelona's fishermen have lived for generations. The restaurants line the Passeig de Joan de Borbó, which is the busy four-lane highway that connects Barcelona to the beaches of La Barceloneta and the Mediterranean Sea. The highway separates La Barceloneta from Port Vell and its mile-long collection of superyachts. On La Barceloneta side, the back streets and alleyways are filled with floor upon floor of tiny balconies with clothing hung out to dry, hanging between the flags of Catalonia and those of FC Barcelona football. Think New York City in the early 1900s. Quite a paradox with the glistening yachts just across the main thoroughfare.

Along the wide, sunny sidewalk of Passeig de Joan de Borbó sit stretches of tables, their umbrellas fluttering in the light breeze from the sea. The passing crowds are full of energy, laughter and song, and the fresh fish is so appealing with a glass of crisp Spanish white wine.

Seafood paella is all of their specialties. You can't go to Barcelona without sampling its most famous dish. That marvelous creation dominates many of the tables. Delivered in an enormous, sizzling cast-iron skillet, it nearly covers your table. You are greeted by its enchanting aroma even before it arrives. A wonderful dish of rice, clam broth, onion, garlic, paprika, artichokes, rosemary, pieces of baby squid, mussels, shrimp, and topped with a gigantic crayfish. It can feed your entire table, and it often does. (Lisa always had to turn the giant crayfish away from her so she would not have to look into its eyes.) We loved all of these restaurants as well.

In the labyrinths of backstreets behind the main drag is another collection of fascinating restaurants with a mostly local clientele. The blackboard menus are in Catalan. The only way to order was to point and hope for the best.

Most of these tiny restaurants probably look as they did 50 years ago. No signs. Uncomfortable, small, wobbly tables and chairs. Tired-looking tile floors. Dusty framed fishing pictures from decades ago. Wines delivered in unmarked reusable glass bottles accompanied by water glasses in mix-and-match style. The kitchen is staffed by the mother, father, grandfather and grandmother. But you are guaranteed great home-cooked meals. Often seafood as well, but simpler. One of the staples on the side is the bomba, a ball of potatoes filled with meat and a spicy sauce or aioli. La Cova Fumada and Can Maño are often completely filled within 10 minutes of opening. No reservations. Get there exactly on time. Wandering guitar players filter in and out looking for change. A blast from the past. Great fun.

Yet the most fun in Barcelona for eating and drinking is "tapas-hopping." The objective is not to have a main dish at all, just an appetizer and a glass of wine or beer at multiple places all around town. Every neighborhood of Barcelona has probably hundreds of bars for tapas-hopping, but everyone really knows the two or three great ones and they are always packed. Lisa and I would look them up on their websites to see how crowded they were at that moment to determine if we could even get in. We found one or two per neighborhood that we returned to again and again. The bartenders and servers got to know us. Unlike at many American bars and restaurants, these people love their jobs. They love their customers, most of whom are regulars. They love to joke with them and tease them. We loved it. These guys and girls could even predict what we were going to order. Just so predictable.

In the core of La Barceloneta are El Vaso de Oro, Jai-Ca and La Bombeta.

El Vaso de Oro is packed with a fascinating mixture of office workers in business attire, people coming from the gym in athletic gear, and construction workers straight from the work site. Almost all locals. It is busy and boisterous, and only Catalan is spoken. Nearly everyone sits or stands at the bar. A low-slung glass cooler runs the length of the bar with an incredible selection of Russian salad, spicy tuna, anchovies and much more. The grill in the corner cooks up sirloin with foie gras and sandwiches of cheese and Spanish ham. The bartenders in their sea captain uniforms are always laughing and busting their customers' chops, including ours. The preferred drink here is home brewed beer. In the evening, when we were in doubt, this is where we came.

La Bombeta has the best bombas in Barcelona. They also are known for fried fish, grilled octopus and grilled squid. It's always packed, but you can take out from the window on the street.

In the El Born neighborhood, Cal Pep, El Xampanyet and La Vinya del Senyor are where to go.

Cal Pep opens at 1 p.m. and again at 7:30. If you get there at its opening time, the line is already around the corner, and the place is filled five minutes later. Great tuna tartare, razor clams, fried artichokes, mushrooms with pesto, and Spanish omelets. If you are unsure what to order, they just start bringing you things until you tell them to stop. Great fun.

El Xampanyet is equally crazy. It is across from the Picasso Museum. The line forms before they open at 7. It is small, cramped and very loud. The smiling bartenders look like NFL linemen and speak no English. We became friends with two of them, even though we spoke no Catalan. How did we communicate? Hand signs and funny faces. You just yell and point into their wall-to-wall cold table at what you would like. They're also known for their house-made cava, a sparkling wine. Everyone has a bottle and a few glasses in front of them on the bar, or on the side tables, or balanced awkwardly under their arm. Everything is excellent here: wide varieties of anchovies, grilled squid with tomato and garlic, razor clams, potato omelets with chorizo, ham croquettes. It is an authentic experience not to be missed.

La Vinya del Senyor is the number one wine bar in Barcelona. It has an extensive wine list and very knowledgeable bartenders who love to educate you on the wonderful range of wines Spain has to offer. Again, Lisa came to know everything about their lives. It sits across the Plaça de Santa Maria from a 14th-century Gothic cathedral. Great cheese and Iberian ham plates. Great sausages from all over Spain as well. A great place to just sit back and relax.

In El Poble-sec, it is Quimet & Quimet, a quirky little tapas bar with extraordinary food. Salmon yogurt and honey truffle sandwich. Blue cheese and roasted peppers. Artichokes and caviar. Great mussels and anchovies. Always packed as well. You're lucky if you can secure one of their small stand-up tables and camp out.

In the Gothic Quarter, there are the Box and Milk. The Box is a funky and funny little place, with "Looney Tunes" cartoons playing all afternoon and evening. Their flavored rum drinks are infused with banana, apple cinnamon, pineapple or ginger. The best guacamole hot dogs in Barcelona. A wide range of Latin American tapas. Always hopping. The owner and his wife became friends as well.

On La Barceloneta beach, try Moma Beach Bar, Bar del Mar and La Deliciosa. They are all right on the edge of the beach. Cava and simple foods. Great breeze. Great people watching. You can sit there all day, with or without an umbrella, and just enjoy the beautiful Mediterranean gently slapping at the sand.

Tapas-hopping is clearly the way to go in Barcelona. If we went at night, we'd occasionally fall prey to a plate of sardines, the octopus with paprika and olive oil, or squid in a spicy tomato sauce. But at lunchtime it balanced our budget and offset our expensive French restaurants.

BARCELONA CANNABIS CLUBS

After Amsterdam, Barcelona has become another very popular "weed-cation" destination in Europe. With over 200 legal private cannabis clubs, it has developed a reputation for both a great cannabis selection and a relaxed, friendly environment. Many locals join three to five clubs based on where they are in the city and what they are looking for. The clubs range from large affairs spread over three floors with bars, DJs, movies and Sony PlayStations to bare-bones one-room basements. The clubs have funny and eclectic names: God Save the Weed, Dragon Cannabis Club, Sticky Born, Cool High and many crazy others.

You need to be invited to join. For many it is as simple as applying on a website. Others need a referral from a current member, which can also be straightforward if you google them and ask a member to sponsor you. When you arrive, you need to present your passport, driver's license and a local address. The membership fee is as low as 10 euros and can be as high as €100 but averages €20 or €30.

Smoking marijuana in your home or in these clubs is legal in Barcelona. Smoking in public is illegal and can result in a fine or arrest, so members need to be careful after they leave the club.

Lisa and I joined three clubs. We spent most of our time in one club, Circulo. It was in the section of Barcelona called El Born and close to our favorite wine bar (La Vinya del Senyor), favorite pizzeria (La Pizza del Born), and favorite tapas bars in El Born (El Xampanyet) and in La Barceloneta (El Vaso de Oro). I don't know what came first, the chicken or the egg. Did they become our favorites because we always went to our favorite cannabis club first?

Circulo has a wide variety of pre-rolled joints, hashish and edibles. The edible that was most fun was cannabis gummy bears. Sounds silly, but they were very effective for walking about town and indulging unnoticed.

Lisa chose not to get high again after Amsterdam. Circulo has a bar that serves a very good Spanish white wine, so she was always happy. It has a great DJ all day and night, and the crowd is young, friendly, diverse and fun. We just chilled on their comfortable couches with our associates when we were there. We went once or twice (or maybe more) a week.

The highlight of our club experience was when we brought our friends from the United States who had joined us to stay in our Airbnb. We stopped by and obtained brownie edibles for all of us and headed out to El Vaso de Oro. Jack is a 66-year-old retired college professor and academic writer with a Ph.D. in international affairs, and Barbara is a 66-year-old minister with a Ph.D. in religious studies. We knew each other from college, and they hadn't gotten high since then, 45 years before. They had become relatively careful and cautious since they reached their 60s. Now it was brownie time in Barcelona for Jack and Barbara.

At El Vaso de Oro, we started relaxed over beers and eventually filled our table with a number of tapas specialties. Then the brownies kicked in. The sirloin steak and seared foie gras was the best meal Jack had ever tasted. No, the spicy tuna was. The Russian salad was the best he'd ever had. The patatas-bravas was the best. No, the croquettes. No, the grilled Spanish ham and cheese was the best he ever had. It went on for over an hour. Everything was the best dish Jack and Barbara had ever tasted.

Eventually we wandered, staggered, sauntered, swirled home. When we were settled in our living room, everything Lisa said was the funniest thing Jack and Barbara had ever heard. They were hysterical. After an hour of uncontrolled laughter, they wandered

Architecture and
Art in Barcelona

B arcelona has been the home of three great Western artists:
Gaudí, Picasso and Miró.

The works of Antoni Gaudí, the best-known practitioner of
Catalan Modernism, are everywhere in the city. His work spans
the genres of architecture, ceramics, stained glass and wrought-iron
forging. He is one of a kind. His major works include La Sagrada
Familia basilica, the apartment building Casa Milà (also known as
La Pedrera for its resemblance to a stone quarry), Park Güell, the
Casa Batlló museum and event space, and the Palau Güell mansion.
They have been all granted World Heritage status by Unesco.

La Sagrada Familia is Gaudí's most visited work, with over three
million visitors a year. In fact, it is the second-most visited site in
Spain (after the Alhambra). Begun in 1882, it will not be finished
until 2026, the 100th anniversary of Gaudí's death. Its decorative
elements are targeted for completion in 2032. When finally done,
after 150 years, it will have 18 towers: one for Jesus Christ, one for
the Virgin Mary, four for the evangelists and 12 for the apostles.

The church has been described as breathtaking, bizarre, beautiful,
spiritual, quirky, whimsical and hideous. There is nothing like it in
the history of the architecture and art of churches. Although Gaudí
was responsible for the original design, the different architects who
built each of the three facades — Nativity to the east, Passion to the
west and Glory to the south — worked in very different sculptural
styles. Buy a book on the church upon your arrival to understand

what exactly you are looking at and what it represents. It is all very, very unusual. Also, pick a sunny day for your visit, and watch how the sun, as it moves across the sky, plays on the purples, greens and oranges of the stained-glass windows, shifting the colors in the towering sanctuary.

Casa Milà, with its rough, undulating limestone facade and twisting wrought-iron balconies, was built between 1906 and 1912 as a private residence. Its most fascinating architectural and sculptural feature is its roof, which is a landscape of hills and valleys. On the rooftop terrace are six skylight/staircase exits and 28 tall, sculpted chimneys, which Gaudí decorated as "espanta bruixes" or witch scarers. These theatrical sculptures are fascinating, borderline frightening. The entire landscape has been called the garden of warriors. Another bizarre Gaudí work of art.

Casa Batlló is another Gaudí masterpiece. The roof is a dragon's back. The balconies in the forms of carnival masks are the skulls of the dragon's victims. Its local nickname is Casa del Ossos or House of the Bones. The remarkable facade has a swirling pattern of repeating pastel colors.

Park Güell, a public park on Carmel Hill, was created between 1900 and 1914. Its most prominent visual element is Gaudí's multicolored mosaic salamander, known as "the dragon," at the park's entrance. It was featured in Woody Allen's film "Vicky Cristina Barcelona" as a target of Vicky's exploration of the city. Another wonderful element is the long bench in the form of a sea serpent that serves as the main terrace at the top of the park and has great views of the city.

Gaudí's body of work is amazing, unconventional, unorthodox and eccentric. In his day, the late 1800s and early 1900s, nothing like it had ever been seen or done before. Much of it was mocked during his lifetime. But it has stood the test of time. We loved all of his creations, but they were collectively so weird that we thought that possibly they were meant to be observed when you were high on marijuana. Maybe.

Picasso spent his early years here, between 1890 and 1917. The Picasso Museum houses the world's largest collection — 3,500 selections — of his early work, hung sequentially. It gives an interesting perspective and insight on how his work evolved over the years. We finally understood who influenced Picasso and how he developed. There are important works from his blue, rose, neo-classic and analytical cubist periods. The "Las Meninas" series, which is a suite of cubist interpretations of a famous painting by Velazquez, are fascinating. They fill an entire room. Picasso spent most of his illustrious career in Paris, where there is another dedicated museum, and ended it in the South of France, which has yet another dedicated museum in Antibes, but Barcelona holds an important collection of his work. We loved them all.

The Fundació Joan Miró, on the top of the mountain of Montjuic, contains 14,000 of his paintings, sketches and sculptures. It was founded by Miró himself in 1975. He was an amazing artist, and although his work has been categorized as surrealistic because it explores the subconscious, in reality it is undefinable. He was in a school of his own. His early works were influenced by the Cubists and the Surrealists, but he developed a language all his own in his unique approach to painting, sculpture and ceramics. A careful examination of his work will show the influence he had on the Abstract Expressionists who followed him like Rothko, Pollock and Motherwell. This is just a fun, fascinating and joyful collection of his quirky work. Take your time here and savor his unconventional approach to art and sculpture.

Actually, on second thought, if you look at the common elements of Gaudí's most unusual work, Picasso's "synthetic cubism" phase, and Miró's surrealist work, maybe they were all meant to be experienced high? Just maybe.

Sevilla

L isa was dying to get started with the Feria de Abril de Sevilla, or April Fair of Seville. Our taxi was crawling through the tiny one-way back streets on the way to our Airbnb. April Fair is a six-day party that captivates the city every year. The locals live all year for the dancing, drinking, eating and socializing of Feria de Abril. The party starts at 1:30 p.m. and most days goes all night until the next morning. It is held in the Los Remedios district in the southwest of the city, near the River Guadalquivir. The enormous fairgrounds are thickly packed with 1,000 casetas, highly decorated tents, across 12 crisscrossed streets. The event actually dominates the entire city, not just that area, with couples in elaborately decorated horse-drawn carriages, men on horseback and everyone else walking around in their traditional Feria de Abril outfits. For women, that means elaborate "trajes de flamenca" (flamenco-style) dresses, and for men, the equally elaborate "trajes de corto" (short jacket, tight pants and boots), or their best suits. The back of Los Remedios is filled by an enormous amusement park along Calle del Infierno, or Hell Street, where the Sevillanos' children spend their evenings. Lisa had hoped that this week would be the highlight of her entire trip. She would soon find out.

Our cab finally stopped at a nondescript intersection with no street names or house numbers. The driver began talking to us in Spanish and taking our luggage out of the trunk. We assumed he was telling us we were there, at our Airbnb. But where was there? We asked which way we should walk, but failed to get an answer we could understand before he jumped back into the taxi and disappeared down the road. We looked at each other uneasily and randomly dragged our bouncing wheelie suitcases down the cobblestones toward an old church. We approached a number of people along the way, inquired where we needed to go, and finally found out it was in the opposite direction. Not an auspicious start. We turned around, bounced back up the hill, reached the top, and bounced down the other side. We finally located our place. It had double wooden doors 20 feet high with a large brass kick plate.

We rang the bell and a man answered. We explained who we were and he smiled broadly and welcomed us to Seville and the Feria de Abril. We followed him into a large sun-drenched courtyard. The second floor was lined with flower pots hanging from an attractive wrought-iron railing, and the ground floor was filled with palm trees, other trees and ferns and flowering plants. The floor itself was a checkerboard pattern of black and white tiles. Wow. This Airbnb might exceed our expectations.

We crossed the courtyard and followed the man up the long stairway to the second floor. When we entered our room, a plumber was in the bathroom. Not a good sign. He explained to us he that was fixing the system because the prior residents had complained there was no water pressure. Not again, Mr. Airbnb.

By the time our host explained to Lisa how everything worked, the plumber was done and everything was fixed. We sighed in relief.

We quickly unpacked and hurried back out to begin to explore the town. At the end of our tiny, pedestrian-only street, we turned the corner and accidentally ran into the biggest flamenco outfit store in all of Seville. Perfect.

After encouraging Lisa multiple times, I persuaded her go in. The store sold only flamenco outfits. These dresses are body-hugging to the mid-thigh, and then continue in multiple layers of ruffles to the ankle. The layers fan out widely from the skirt and the sleeves. The outfit is completed with a "manton de Manila" shawl. Accessories include a decorative comb, artificial flowers and a matching multicolored fan.

Lisa slowly flipped through the brightly colored dresses. There were floral patterns and polka dots. Red with big white dots, black with white dots, red with black dots, pink with small white dots, blue with small blue dots, yellow with tiny yellow dots, the variations were limitless. The brightly colored patterned dresses have a limitless set of alternatives as well, pink and green floral, coral and violet floral. It was incredible.

Then Lisa looked at the prices. Also incredible. They started at around 300 euros and went to over €500. She said forget it. I explained to her that she had to buy one. How could she spend six days in this beautiful sun-drenched Spanish city of endless music, dancing and parties and not have one of these dresses? After feigned disagreement, she began trying them on. The saleswoman helped her with one after another.

She tried on a pink, yellow and green floral dress with a light blue background that extended in layers and layers of ruffles to her ankles and her sleeves. She looked in the mirror and lit up in a glowing smile. Then her whole face lit up. The saleswoman returned with the matching comb and fan and put the comb and a white artificial flower in Lisa's hair, which was already in a bun. The saleswoman added large matching pink hoop earrings as well. Lisa spun around in the mirror. Again that radiant glow surrounded her. She said she looked like a princess. She said she had never had a princess dress before. A 58-year-old princess, but a princess nonetheless. I never knew that all women have this dream of being a princess. All their lives.

We paid up, packed her old clothes into a shopping bag that I carried out, and took off to conquer Seville. We were surprised to see that although the festival didn't start for a few hours, the local women were already out in their finest flamenco outfits. Everywhere. It was a kind of "Wizard of Oz"-like atmosphere. At Disneyland only the characters wear costumes, but in Seville, everyone does. We wandered around town a bit and returned home.

I had to take countless pictures of Lisa in the dress to send to her sisters and girlfriends. She was pirouetting in the courtyard of our Airbnb, curving her arms around her head and body with that bent flamenco dancer's elbow that you typically see. Pictures. Dancing on the second-floor balcony, spinning and weaving. Pictures. It was hysterical. We dropped off her old clothes, I put on my suit, and we headed off to the fair.

Beautifully dressed couples passed us in decorated horse-drawn carriages. Four-horse carriages, six-horse carriages with two couples each. Each more elaborately decorated than the first. The clopping sound of carriage after carriage and the sheer beauty of all of the horses, carriages and participants created an enormous sense of energy. We were dying to arrive at this event.

We crossed the Guadalquivir River and finally arrived and entered the fairgrounds. They were already packed with people. The swirling sea of women in flamenco outfits was an undulating kaleidoscope of colors. The sun was setting and the streetlights were lit with string after string of alternating white and yellow lanterns. The streets are all named for famous bullfighters. The energy of the place was crazy.

We entered our first caseta. It was on the front edge of the fairgrounds and possibly the largest tent there. It was open to the public. Flamenco music was being played by a big band on the stage, which was also filled by a large group of women in their colorful dresses, spinning and dancing. We went to the bar behind the stage and bought sherries, a small cheese plate and two small ham croquetas, and went back to the front of the stage and grabbed a table. The music and dancing were intoxicating.

After two more sherries, Lisa was ready for the stage. She jumped up and began to weave herself into the middle of the group. She swayed around watching the women on either side and immediately absorbed their moves. Song by song, she became synchronized with the best of them and soon was dancing with her arms arching.

Swirling, spinning, heels stomping. It was pretty amazing. My little Spanish princess.

We eventually left that first tent and toured the rest of the fairgrounds. It felt like a real village. Each tent is a different private club, or trade association, prominent Seville family, political party, or just group of friends. They save all year to pay for this weeklong party, so most of them are closed to the public. Every tent has a band of its own, a stage, dancing, food and drink. It also has a bouncer. Of the thousand casetas, there are probably only eight large tents open to the public, but they are the largest. We went to another two before we began to feel exhausted and headed home. It was great people-watching. Families, groups of girlfriends talking loudly and laughing, groups of boys pushing each other back and forth, each at their own large oval table. Only the women dance, as is the custom. What fun everyone seemed to be having. What an amazing event, this Feria de Abril de Sevilla.

When we finally arrived home, Lisa took her flamenco outfit off to go to bed. The next morning, we awoke, went to the gym, came home, had a cup of coffee, and she put the flamenco dress back on. That day was the opening of the Plaza de Toros de la Real Maestranza de Caballería de Sevilla, site of the best-known bullfighting festivals in the world.

The 12,000-capacity Seville bullring is a grand circular coliseum that was finished in 1881 and is two-thirds stone and one-third wood with a beautiful Baroque facade. It is divided by four major arches and three tiers of seats that include a box for the Spanish royal family, and is topped off by a blue and white tiled roof.

Lisa was a bit reluctant to attend, but we agreed to leave after the first bullfight if it disturbed her. Quite a royal festival it was. The overflow crowd was dressed in their festival best. Just as many people focused their cameras and binoculars on the stands as on the ring. It was glorious. In the end, Lisa decided it was too gory for her, and we did indeed leave after the first fight. But not without many more photos of her in the stands in her dress.

We now knew that many people didn't head straight to the fair but instead crossed the Guadalquivir River on a closer bridge, the iconic Isabel II, and cut through the Triana neighborhood, which has clusters of tapas bars. This area is packed with ceramics stores and atmospheric places where locals eat and drink. We stopped at a few and it was fun and inexpensive.

We then followed the crowds back to another afternoon at the festival. We left early to attend an authentic flamenco show, where Lisa took notes and kicked her heels in her seat along with the dancers.

The next morning began the same way: gym, coffee, put on the flamenco dress. We went to explore the immense Seville Cathedral and La Giralda, its bell tower. One of the largest churches in Europe after St. Peter's in Rome, its construction began in 1401 and took over a century to complete. The interior is striking with its Gothic vaulted ceiling rising 184 feet above the transept. It has an elegant Renaissance dome. The extraordinary main chapel is carved with scenes from the life of Christ and is gleaming with gold leaf. The bell tower is 322 feet tall and has a gently sloping ramp that allows you to climb to the top for an excellent view of the city. It is topped by a bronze weathervane sculpture depicting faith.

The next morning, gym, coffee, flamenco dress, old town Triana, and back to the festival. Glorious Spanish music pouring out of every tent. Dancing in the tents. Dancing in the streets. Lisa was proud to have sneaked into multiple private tents. She was a Sevillana now, dancing among all of them. The energy everywhere was incredible, again.

The next day, the same.

The next day, no dress. We went to the medieval town of Córdoba. A short train ride brought us to the convergence of the Roman, Moorish, Jewish and Christian civilizations. During much of the Middle Ages, when Spain was under Muslim rule, Muslims, Christians and Jews lived side by side and enriched each other intellectually and culturally. The wondrous iconic representation of that era is the Mezquita, the Córdoba Mosque-Cathedral. The mihrab, or prayer niche, and the forest of 850 marble columns and horseshoe-shaped stone arches striped in the color sienna, are jewels of Muslim architecture. When the Christians eventually defeated the Muslims, they preserved this incredibly beautiful mosque and placed a cathedral in its center. It contains beautiful Baroque choir stalls and two pulpits of marble, jasper and mahogany. What a wondrous weaving together of religious designs. A treasure.

We returned to Seville to put on the dress for one last night of glorious celebration. The next morning the event was over. Flamenco costumes were to be returned to storage. Not ours. Lisa put it on for one last morning on the town. We walked to the Alfonso XIII, a landmark luxury hotel, for a last glorious Bloody Mary-fueled brunch. Lisa was the only one still wearing the dress. From there, we went on a leisurely horse and carriage ride through the beautiful Parque Maria Luisa, which was erected for the Ibero-American Exposition of 1929. The park is with filled with trees, fountains and flower gardens. We crossed the semicircular Plaza de España, the centerpiece of the 1929 exposition, and returned to the Alfonso XIII. More photos in the carriage with Lisa's big fan held out in front of her.

When Lisa stepped down from the carriage, a large tourist bus pulled up, and a number of older Italian women scrambled out. They were looking for the flamenco dancers, unaware that the fair had ended the previous evening. Then they spotted Lisa in her dress. They flocked over and surrounded her, clucking and making a fuss. One woman and then another jumped out in front of the group and started taking pictures with Lisa in the front and center of the entire crowd, a smiling, happy, laughing group. It went on for 10 or 15 minutes. They were sure they had captured an authentic Spaniard in her party dress. Lisa remained silent so as to not disturb their ecstatic frenzy. As they finally wandered off, she now knew what is was like to be a princess.

WE FOUND OURSELVES

We'd never planned on shortening our travels by two months. But we did, and it felt fortunate. On April 3, 2017, a bomb in the St. Petersburg metro killed 15 people and injured 45. We had assumed it would be the safest city on that segment of our trip.

After my mom's death and funeral, we had significant responsibilities because I was the executor of her estate. We needed to list her homes for sale in Florida and New Jersey, pay her final bills, close her accounts, discontinue all of her cable, telephone, cellphone, gas, electric and other services, transfer her assets, sell her cars and much more, all from Barcelona.

This required using a Spanish notary, the equivalent of a lawyer in many ways. We met in a high-ceilinged room with shelves packed with law books and an enormous oak desk. Every document was drafted in both English and Spanish. We needed translators to ensure we understood all the formalities, and the meetings often lasted for hours. We sent paperwork to lawyers and real estate agents back home. These meetings exhausted us, and took up much of the time we were going to spend planning the last three months of our journey. In the end, we just called an audible. We decided to spend a month at Lisa's sister's vacation home on the beach in Nice, France. Just chill in the warm, relaxing Mediterranean sun. Then go home.

When we got back, we found that the world had shifted in subtle ways. Our extended absence had had an impact on our children. Even though we had talked to each of them once a week, they also called each other to stay connected as a family. They got together for Thanksgiving and Easter to cook for each other as a team. They had never done that before. That responsibility was always Lisa's. As a result, they became closer than they had ever been. It truly surprised us, and it was beautiful to watch from afar.

We wondered why it happened. Maybe they were worried we would never return. That sounds crazy, but we did experience a number of earthquakes in Italy. There were terrorist attacks in Paris and Barcelona while we were there. There were forest fires close to us in Nice and across southern France. Maybe their wonderful spirit of connectedness was just meant to be. And with our condo still rented, we stayed with our son for a while.

We were still eager to soak up the history of Western art, and to see the best pieces that were in our backyard. We went to New York and visited the Museum of Modern Art and the Metropolitan Museum to see what we had missed. MoMA has van Gogh's magnificent "Starry Night" and many more. The Met has Manet's "Boating" and "The Dance Class" by Degas. We traveled to the National Gallery of Art and the Phillips Collection in Washington, and in Philadelphia we visited the Barnes Foundation and the Philadelphia Museum of Art. The Barnes has 181 Renoirs, 69 Cézannes, 59 Matisses and 46 Picassos, all a 10-minute walk from our home. Unbelievable.

I signed up for seven courses at the Barnes to better comprehend what we had just experienced. A 14-week course called "Collection Concentration: Renoir" examined the entire history of his work. I still wanted to understand it all.

Then we just stopped and took deep, long breaths. Chilled. Reflected on our entire experience. Discussed what had just happened to us. And then we had the epiphany. It wasn't about the thread of our art experiences, our cultural experiences, epicurean experiences, personal connections to the locals in Europe, none of it. The most important thing that happened on our adventure was between Lisa and me.

We had devoted months to planning our journey. We'd been motivated and intoxicated about so many aspects of the trip. Once we arrived and spent every day, week after marvelous week, wandering each city, we exceeded our expectations. And the most amazing thing was that we began to change. In becoming Romans and Parisians and Catalonians, we lost our regrets, our jealousies, our scar tissue of frustrating jobs and missed opportunities, the friendship and relationship disappointments, and the things we had hoped would happen in our lives and never did. We became like children, appreciating everything as if for the first time, every meal, every glass of wine, the surprise of yet another stain-glassed, sun-splashed church, a protest march around the next corner led by a flag-draped megaphone, the countless talented street musicians, mimes and the occasional opera singer. We lost ourselves in this new home.

In pursuing this odyssey, we also found ourselves. We had followed the history of Western art from city to city, artist to artist, genre to genre. We had traveled from ancient Rome to the Middle Ages and on to Gothic churches, the Renaissance, the Baroque, Neoclassicism, Impressionism, Cubism and Surrealism. The love of art and architecture transfixed and seized our minds and our souls. We rediscovered the Enlightenment in Paris and reaffirmed how it was the foundation of the American experiment in democracy. We found a society whose heroes were philosophers who were enshrined in the greatest monuments. We followed great writers through their cafés and restaurants We bought their books and reread them and bathed in them as if we had just met them for the first time.

We found ourselves through art, philosophy, literature and rediscovering each other. We reinvented who we were. I became patient, calm and understanding, and Lisa became passionately and obsessively curious about all things. Who influenced whose thinking in these great works, how did that school of art evolve, who inspired the design of this building, how did they know it was mathematically possible to create that amazing dome? She became the most self-assured, adventurous and outgoing that I had ever seen her. And Lisa lived, for the first time, entirely in the moment. We both did.

We lost ourselves and we found ourselves at the same time.

Raising three healthy, happy children is the greatest bonding experience two people can ever have. After that, spending 24 hours a day together for 10 months has the potential to make or break a couple. In our case, it turned out to be remarkable. First, we didn't kill each other, even if that sometimes appeared possible. Second, we really got to understand each other. Seriously. For both the good and the not so good.

We learned to anticipate each other's rhythms, cadences and unmet needs, and we could almost foresee and foreshadow each other's thoughts, hopes and fears. Sometimes scary, but mostly good. Very good. As for the make or break, this adventure made us. We were never the same.

Sevilla, Joe and Lisa in carriage

Printed in the United States
By Bookmasters